Poultry Houses, Coops and Equipment
A Book of Plans for the Chicken Raiser

by H.A. Nourse

with an introduction by Jackson Chambers

This work contains material that was originally published in 1906.

This publication is within the Public Domain.

This edition is reprinted for educational purposes
and in accordance with all applicable Federal Laws.

Introduction Copyright 2016 by Jackson Chambers

Introduction

I am pleased to present yet another title on Poultry.

This volume is entitled "Poultry Houses, Coops and Equipments" and was authored by H.A. Nourse in 1906.

The work is in the Public Domain and is re-printed here in accordance with Federal Laws.

As with all reprinted books of this age that are intended to perfectly reproduce the original edition, considerable pains and effort had to be undertaken to correct fading and sometimes outright damage to existing proofs of this title. At times, this task is quite monumental, requiring an almost total "rebuilding" of some pages from digital proofs of multiple copies. Despite this, imperfections still sometimes exist in the final proof and may detract from the visual appearance of the text.

I hope you enjoy reading this book as much as I enjoyed making it available to readers again.

Jackson Chambers

Preface to Third Edition

In this, the third large edition of "Poultry Houses, Coops and Equipment," the editor wishes to express his thanks to his fellow poultrymen for the enthusiastic reception they have accorded this little book. He trusts that it may continue to be helpful and suggestive to those who desire to construct new buildings to house their flocks, and to those who wish to equip their poultry houses with the most convenient and desirable devices.

H. A. NOURSE,

April, 1911.   Editor.

POULTRY HOUSE CONSTRUCTION.

A Discussion of Locations, Foundations, Frames, Walls, Roofs, Floors, Windows, Doors, Ventilators and the Arrangement of Interior Fixtures.

By H. A. Nourse.

It is easier and less expensive to build a poultry house on the most advantageous location and to construct it properly than it is to change it after it is built, to meet the requirements. The matter of location is an important one. Permanent poultry buildings should never be located upon heavy soil if it can be avoided. Such soil is better adapted to other purposes. Light, sandy soil, but not so light that it will not produce a good crop of grass when fertilized, is considered the best on which to build poultry houses and yards. The impurities are driven into such a soil by the rains and the yards are to some extent self-purifying. In high latitudes where the temperature runs very low in winter, protection from heavy winds is very desirable. On that account poultry buildings are located on the south or east side of a hill or rising ground, when such a location is to be had, or on the south or east side of a thick grove of trees.

A poultry house should always face the south or southeast whichever way the land upon which it is built slopes. If it must face either east or west, by all means have it face east for the morning sun is more necessary in the winter than the afternoon sun, though both are desirable and may be obtained when the house faces the south.

Foundations.

A poultry building should rest upon a firm footing both for convenience when building and to prevent the house sagging out of shape later. The very best foundation is made by excavating a trench 3 feet deep beneath the walls of the house and building therein a solid stone wall, cemented on both sides (Fig. 1). The sills may be placed upon this wall and cemented to it, making the building rat proof and preventing any wind from blowing in near the floor. This wall may be made of any stones which are handy. A good and cheaper foundation is made by sinking four foot posts three feet deep in the ground under each corner of the house and one every four or six feet under the walls, between the corner posts. These posts will project one foot above the ground (if the ground is level) and the space between the sills of the house and the earth should be boarded with two-inch planks. nailed to the posts. This will give the sills a bearing not only upon the posts but upon these planks so that they are supported every inch of their length. A corner post with the sills resting upon it is shown in Fig. 2.

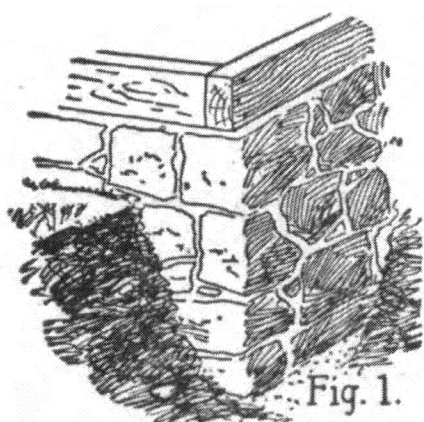
Fig. 1.

Fig. 2.

Frames.

Except in large and heavily constructed houses, light frame work consisting of 2 x 4 and 2 x 3 pieces is sufficient. The sills may be of 2 x 4s if neither of the foundations described above are used. Posts, plates and rafters may be made of the same material while less important parts of the frame will be as satisfactory if 2 x 3s are used. Complicated joints calculated to give additional strength to the frame are seldom necessary for when the building is boarded there is practically no chance of joints pulling apart. The end sills may be spiked to the ends of the front and back sills and the corner posts and up-

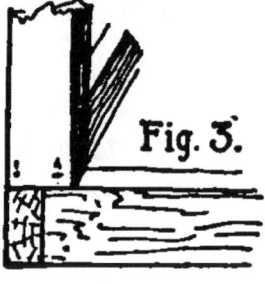
Fig. 3.

right joists may be placed upon the sills and toenailed to them, as shown in Fig. 3. The plates may be nailed between these posts, spiked through the posts into the ends of the plates. The end plates may then be cut and placed between the posts in the manner illustrated by Fig. 4.

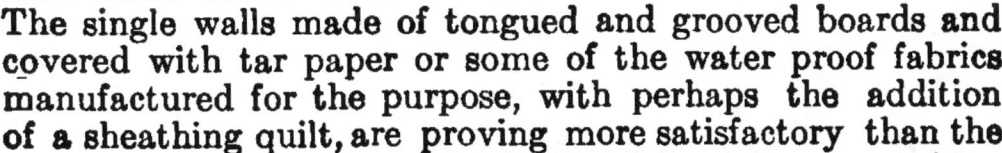

Fig. 4.

Walls.

As time advances poultrymen build fewer double walls. The single walls made of tongued and grooved boards and covered with tar paper or some of the water proof fabrics manufactured for the purpose, with perhaps the addition of a sheathing quilt, are proving more satisfactory than the double walls with a heavy packing of sawdust, earth or hay, which were considered necessary a few years ago.

A good wall, wind and water proof, may be made by covering the frame with tongued and grooved boards, then covering the boards with tar paper and the tar paper in turn with prepared roofing fabric, as shown in Fig. 5. If a double wall is desired, board the outside of the frame as above and after covering the inside with tar paper ceil up with tongued and grooved ceiling stuff. This makes a very tight wall and one which frost will not penetrate during cold weather. This wall has two thicknesses of boards and two of paper. This construction is illustrated in Fig. 6.

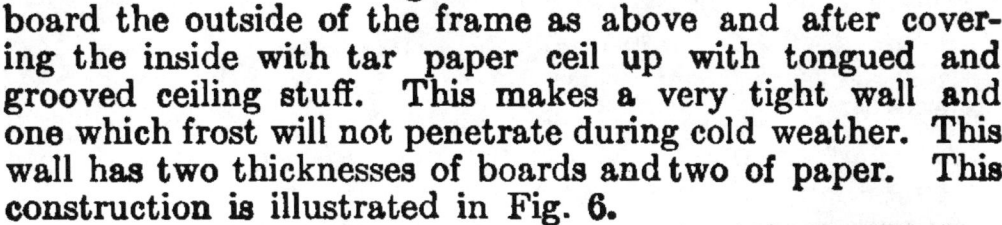

Fig. 5.

Roofs.

A leaky roof is the poultryman's abomination, but with the many brands of prepared roofing now on the market there is no excuse for leaky poultry houses except the inability of the owner to properly apply these fabrics. A shingle roof should

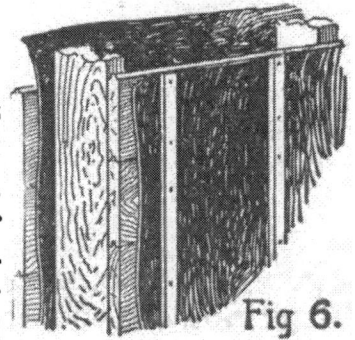

Fig 6.

not be used unless the roof has a considerable slant; prepared roofing is not only cheaper but makes a tighter house. The roof boards should be laid close together and covered with tar paper. Upon the tar paper the roofing fabric should be laid with the strips running lengthwise of the roof. The seams should be well nailed or cemented, or both, and the roof cleated with inch strips ⅝ of an inch thick, placed not more than fifteen inches apart. The roofing fabric should be allowed to project over the roof on all sides enough so that it may be bent down under the eaves and brought against the sides and ends of the house. If it is cleated firmly to the sides and ends (see Fig. 7) it will prevent any wind getting into the house above the plates.

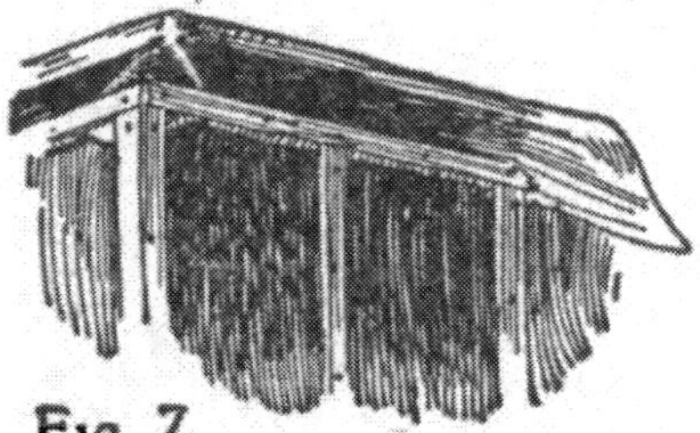

Fig. 7.

Floors.

There is no floor equal to an earth one in the opinion of the writer. The building should be filled in to the bottom of the sills with earth which should then be covered with four inches of coarse sand. As the sills should always be a foot above the sod, this will bring the floor well above the ground outside and will insure freedom from dampness on its surface. If the building sits in a slight depression which would cause water to work under it, it should be banked on the outside. When the foundation is a cement wall this is not necessary. If the nature of the foundation affords opportunity for rats to work through from the outside and burrow up through the earth, fine mesh galvanized wire netting should be placed on the ground, thoroughly covering the space covered by the house, before the earth floor is put in. This may be extended outside and bent up and tacked to the lower part of the house (see Fig. 8), making it rat proof.

Cement floors are useful only when it is necessary to exclude dampness. According to the testimony of most poultry keepers who have used it and according to the writer's experience, cement gives a perceptible chill to the house which is absent when earth floors are used on a well drained location. When a floor is absolutely necessary, in portable houses or houses having a space beneath them to be utilized as exercising room for the fowls, a board floor is the cheapest and is very satisfactory. Although a single thickness of ⅞ inch boards is all that is needed if the house is well banked and the exercising room beneath closely housed in, a double floor with paper between is advisable under other conditions. When banking the house it is not well to bank it absolutely tight; a small place should be left on the south side for ventilation to prevent moisture accumulating under the house and working up through the floor.

Fig. 8.

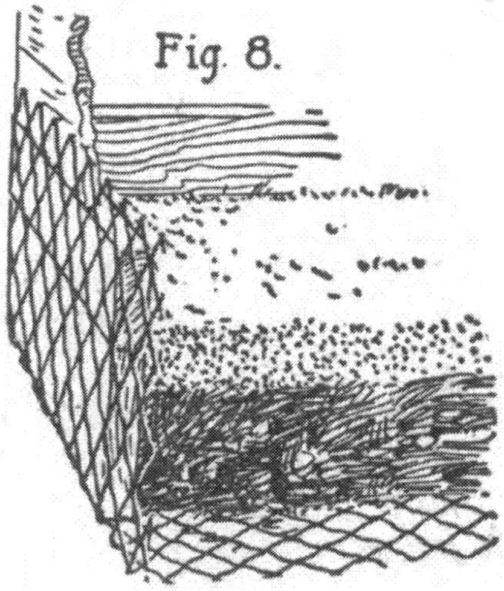

Doors and Windows.

Doors should always be high enough and wide enough so that the person caring for the fowls can go in and out without stooping and can carry through pails of feed or anything used in the work without inconvenience. Outside doors should be located in the end of the house which the caretaker usually approaches when about to care for the fowls. If the house has an alley way or walk the door should open into the alley and not directly into a pen. Doors should be well made and hung on heavy hinges, otherwise they will sag and cease to fit.

Almost all light in a poultry house should be admitted through the south side, though a window in the east end will admit the morning sun and one in the west end will secure the benefit of the last rays in the afternoon. Too much glass is worse than not enough and in a house ten feet wide a full window, containing twelve good sized lights of glass is sufficient for each ten feet of length. All windows should open easily for ventilation and should be well fitted so that when closed they will be wind and water tight.

Ventilators.

Ventilating systems, more or less complicated and in most cases less effective, have been designed to rid the poultry houses of foul air and supply fresh air in return. A majority of these are utterly worthless so far as changing the air is concerned. Houses constructed with solid fronts can be best ventilated by opening and closing the doors and windows and the writer does not know of any system of pipes or flues which he, in justice to himself and his readers, can recommend as useful for the purpose. One of the best

Fig. 9.

ventilators he ever used was made by cutting an aperture above each window in the south side of the house and fitting a cloth filled frame to slide back and forth behind the opening as shown in Fig. 9, which illustrates the manner of attaching the ventilator to the inside of the wall. These frames may be opened in fair weather and closed in stormy or especially severe weather to keep out heavy winds and rain or snow.

Another satisfactory method of admitting fresh air to the house, when the weather will not permit the windows to be opened wide, is to place in the opening made by raising or lowering the windows, cloth filled frames which exactly fill the space, as shown in Fig. 10. Pure air will work through the cloth, but no wind, snow or rain will get through. In buildings of which the south side is wholly or in part cloth, no additional provision for ventilation need be made. Such houses are thoroughly self-ventilating and fowls are usually healthy in such quarters.

Arrangement of Fixtures.

The arrangement of nests, roosts and roost platforms, water pans, etc., is of considerable importance. The location of all of these should be such that the birds may be cared for in the shortest time, therefore for the least expense.

Roosts, if not roost platforms, should be removable

COOPS AND EQUIPMENT. 11

and the latter should be sufficiently high above the floor so that the fowls can exercise under them and no floor space will be lost. Nests may be made singly or in tiers and attached to the sides of the pens or placed under the roost platforms and should always be high enough so that no floor space is covered. Where the building has a walk, birds may be fed, watered, the roost platforms cleaned and the eggs collected without entering the pens. Often times this is a time saver, but many poultrymen believe that the care taker should be in closer touch with his flock than is permitted by this arrangement.

Fig. 10.

COLONY HOUSES

HOUSE FOR TWENTY FOWLS.

A Colony House with Hallway and Other Labor Saving Features.

By F. Leggo, Minnesota.

The accompanying illustrations show plans for building a colony house or a house for one pen of eighteen to twenty fowls. The dimensions are 12 x 14 feet on the ground, outside measurement, 6 feet high on the front or south side, 7 feet high on the rear or north side, and 9 feet high 3½ feet from the rear wall, making the gable over the passage way. The house sits upon a stone foundation and the floor is of dirt. The frame work is of 2 x 4 stuff and the sides and partitions are of unmatched pine boards, dressed on one side and put on with the boards running up and down. The cracks are battened on the outside and the walls are lined with tar paper. The roof is covered with shingles, or, roofing felt may be used.

In the front side are two windows each 24 x 30 inches in size, placed 15 inches from the floor. The house is ventilated by a muslin filled frame placed in an opening 2 x 3 feet in size, located between the windows and three feet from the floor. This opening is also fitted with a wooden door which may be opened or closed, according to the weather.

The entire floor space in the pen is available for scratching, making a scratching floor 8½ x 14 feet. The roosts are 18 inches from the floor. Eighteen inches above the roosts is a platform 3 feet wide on which are the nests, reached by means of a runway or board with cleats nailed on it, as shown in the illustration. Back of the nests is an opening into the passage way, covered with a long board hung on hinges so that the eggs can be gathered from

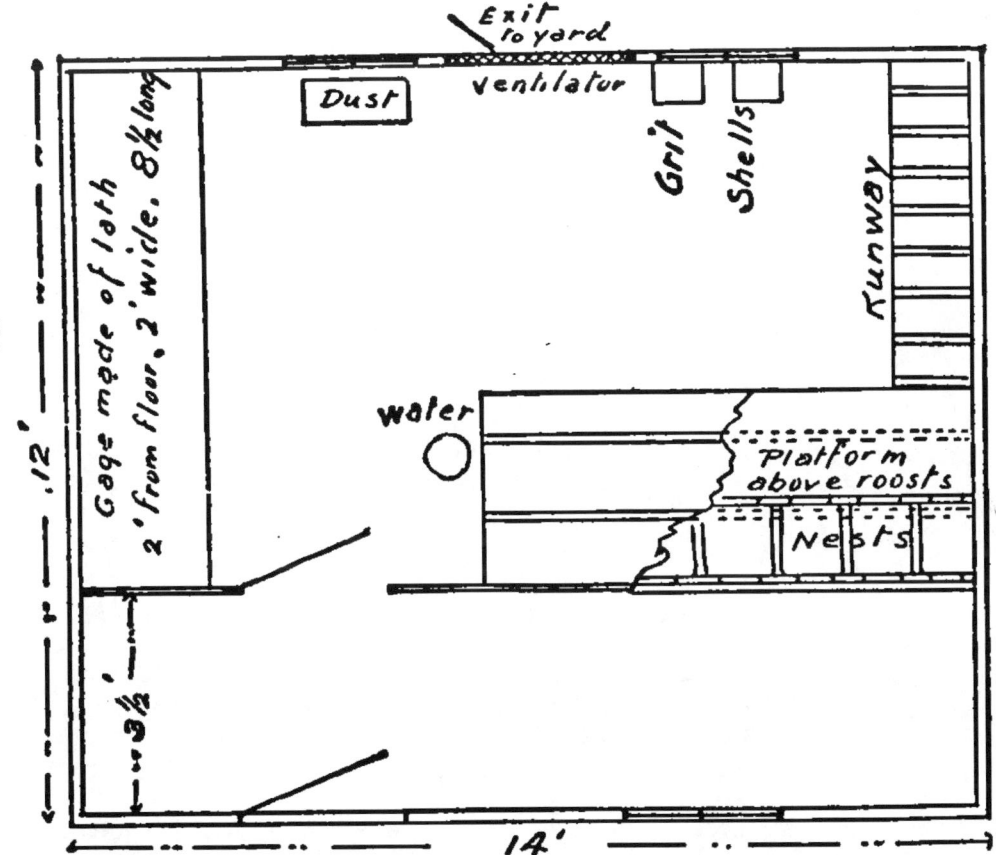

Floor Plan of "House for Twenty Fowls," designed by F. Leggo, Showing the Location of Interior Fixtures and Equipment.

the passage way. The front of the platform has a railing made of lath or wire netting so that the hens have to go up and down the runway and are not likely to hurt themselves flying down to the floor, and so that they will not roost on the platform. In cold weather a curtain is let down from the front and end of the platform in front of and at the end of the roosts at night. In one end of the pen is a cage, 2 feet from the floor and 2 feet wide by 8½ feet long, for surplus males or for breaking up broody hens.

No droppings boards are used; the droppings are mixed with the litter which is raked from under the roosts during the day and changed when necessary. In the passage way there is room for keeping feed, coops, etc., with a window for light as shown in the illustration. Dust bath, grit and shell boxes and water fountain are located as shown in the drawing.

Objection may be made to the absence of droppings

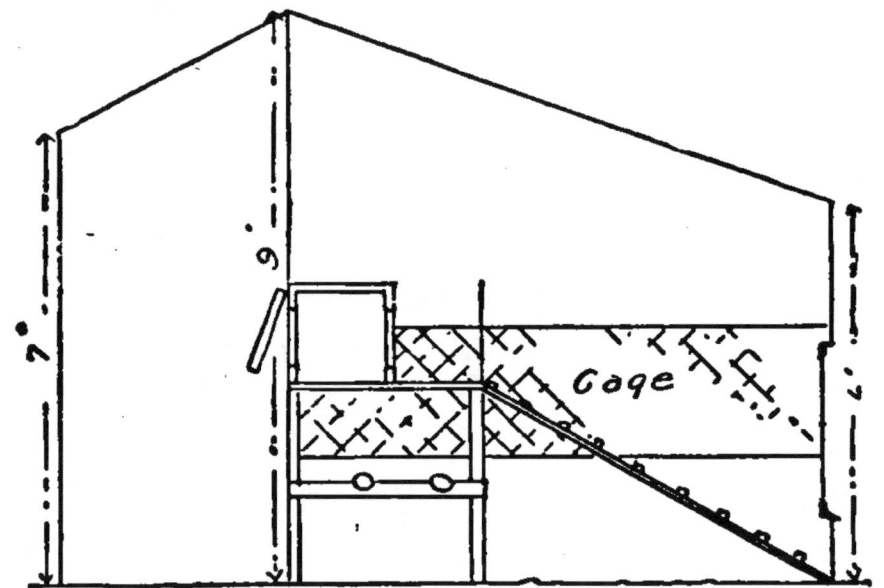

Cross Section of "House for Twenty Fowls," Showing the Location of Roosts, Nests and Runway.

boards. We object to the boards, however, on the ground that the space under them is of no use for scratching and if nests are put under the droppings boards it is so much harder to keep the nests clean. More than that, in handling the droppings we find it much more pleasant when they are diluted with litter.

A COMBINATION COLONY HOUSE.

This House Will Accommodate a Brooder in the Spring and and a Flock of Fowls in the Fall.

By N. J. Holden, Minnesota.

In regard to the plan of the colony house which I herewith present, I will say that I have one exactly like this

Exterior of Colony House, designed by N. J. Holden.

in use and find it convenient to use as a brooder house in the spring. The brooder is placed in the rear and will leave a considerable space in front for an exercising place. I have a ventilating opening fitted with a shutter on each end, near the ceiling, and a large window in the front makes it light and pleasant for the chicks.

I built this house a little expensively. It is made of 4-

inch ceiling, placed vertically, with good tar felt on the inside which is in turn covered with half-inch lumber. This makes it very tight and warm, but the same building can be built of common rough boards with tar felt on the inside which, however, should be stripped with laths and given a coat of whitewash. I would use nothing but boards (no dimension stuff) in the construction of this house if it could be double sheeted. I would fit the boards

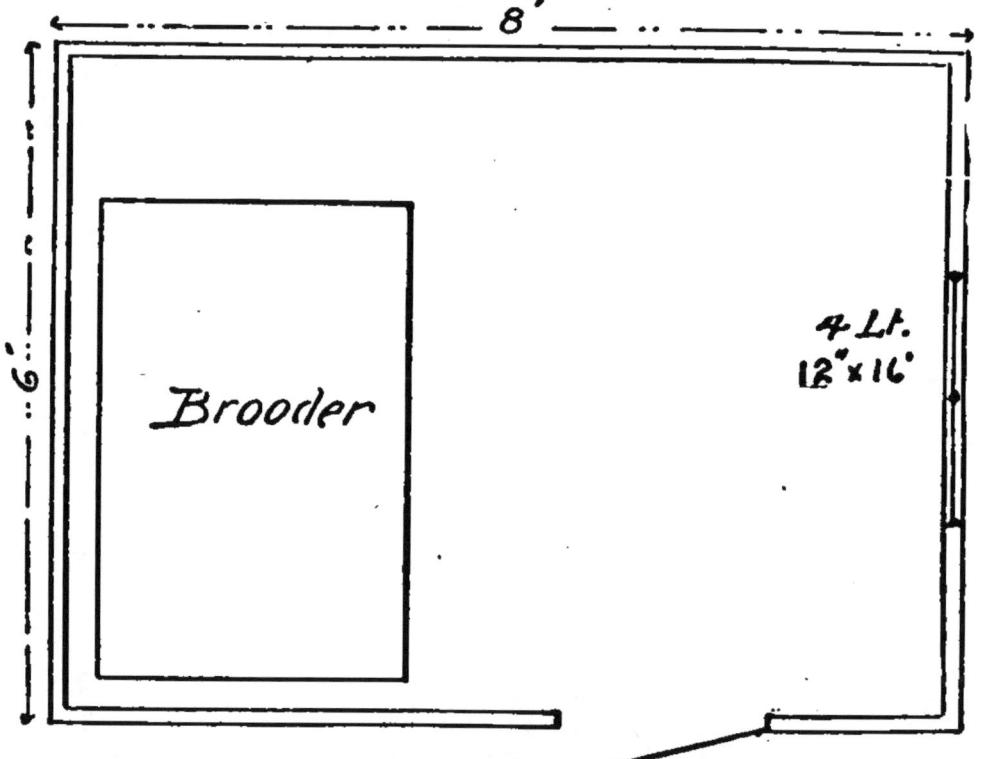

Floor Plan of N. J. Holden's Colony House, Showing Location of Brooder; Roost Platform and Roosts take the place of the Brooder in the Fall.

together firmly making the two ends, front and rear separate, and nail them together at the corners. The outside sheeting should be vertical and the inside horizontal, with paper between. An inch strip should be nailed close to the bottom of the two ends and a couple of 2 x 4 pieces spaced equally between the ends. On these 2 x 4s and the inch strips the floor should be laid. A couple of pieces of 2 x 4 may be used to nail the roof boards to, if desired, and rough boards should be nailed to the tops of the two ends.

A HOUSE WITH ROOSTS NEAR THE FRONT.

A Plan Showing a Novel Arrangement of Interior Fixtures and Construction of Foundation.

By Carrie Blossom, Iowa.

This house is built on a foundation of cedar posts set on double plank imbedded in the ground below frost level. The posts run up to about fourteen inches above the ground where a box sill constructed of two 2 x 6s is spiked to the top of the posts to receive the 2 x 6 floor joists, spaced 16 inches on center. This elevates the building 14 inches above the ground, prevents rats from nesting under the floor and gives a free circulation of air under the building, keeping the floor perfectly dry. During the winter months planks are set against the posts, closing up the openings, and by packing straw or manure against these planks a very warm building is assured.

The building should be built on the north side of the chicken yard so as to form a shelter against the cold north winds. The wall of the south side of the building is four feet high from the floor to the roof and contains three windows, each having twelve lights of 8 x 10 glass. These windows are placed in a vertical position and near the floor, so that in winter when sunshine is most desirable in the building for health and warmth, the sun being lower in the heavens will throw the light far back into the building. In summer, when shade is most desirable, the sun being higher up and the windows near the floor, very little sunshine will be reflected on the floor, keeping the building cool. Between the south windows are two summer doors which in summer are swung up, forming an awning and making the house cool and airy. The north wall is 6 feet high from the floor to the roof, making it high enough for walking upright inside. This wall should be built perfectly storm proof and must contain but few openings; two small

18 POULTRY HOUSES,

windows large enough to give light to see into nests and feed trough are sufficient.

The nests are constructed in two sections as shown at N in the floor plan and in the section. Each section of nests

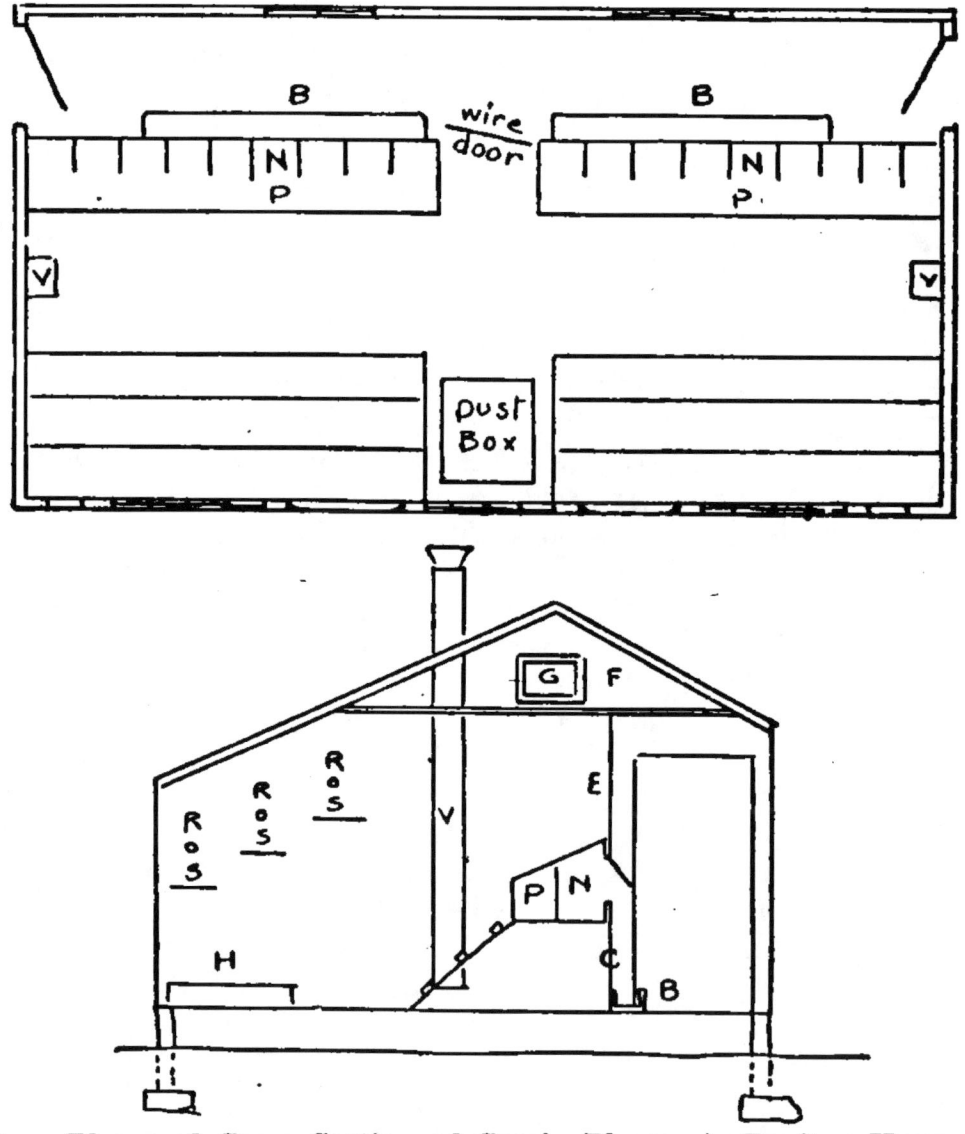

Floor Plan and Cross Section of Carrie Blossom's Poultry House, Indicating Position of Roosts, Nests, etc.

is constructed in one piece, having a passage, P, in front of the nests, and partitions between the nests. The nest boxes can be pulled out separately from the wall, like drawers, for cleaning and refilling with bedding. Back of each nest is a hinged door for the removal of eggs. Each entire section is set on a stationary rack and can be taken out of the building through a door, A, at the end of the section. The nests are covered with a slanted roof to prevent the chickens from roosting on the nests. The bottoms of the nests are eighteen or twenty inches above the floor, to give more floor space to the chickens by allowing them to walk under them to the feed trough, B, which is set in the hall-

Exterior View of Carrie Blossom's Poultry House; note the Swinging Doors in the Front Side for Ventilation.

way against a slat partition, C, constructed of plastering lath spaced so the chickens can reach the food in the trough through the slant partition, but are prevented from soiling the food. These slats are nailed vertically from the floor to the rack which supports the nests. Above the nests to the ceiling is another lath partition, E, and between the two sections of nests is a wire door.

The ceiling is constructed of 6-inch boards, spaced about 2 inches apart. This ceiling is of no use in summer but is very necessary in winter when the triangular space, F, above the ceiling is filled with straw, which greatly adds to the warmth of the building. The ceiling boards are spaced about two inches apart and admit a free circulation of air through the straw and out of slat ventilator, G, indicated in the gable on the drawing of the cross section. Each end of the building is also provided with a vent stack, V, built of 10-inch boards, beginning about 6 or 8 inches above the floor and running up above the highest point of the roof, with board over the top to keep out rain. There are six roost poles, R, which are movable and placed above movable droppings boards, S. H is a dust bath in a box about 3 feet square and 4 inches deep.

A TEN DOLLAR COLONY HOUSE.

A Cheap but Satisfactory Poultry House Designed by a Boy Sixteen Years Old.

By Edwin Daniels, Wisconsin.

I present herewith the plans of a house that I use for one pen of fowls. I have had chickens in it for three years, and have found it very convenient for me and healthful for them. It cost about ten dollars to construct it.

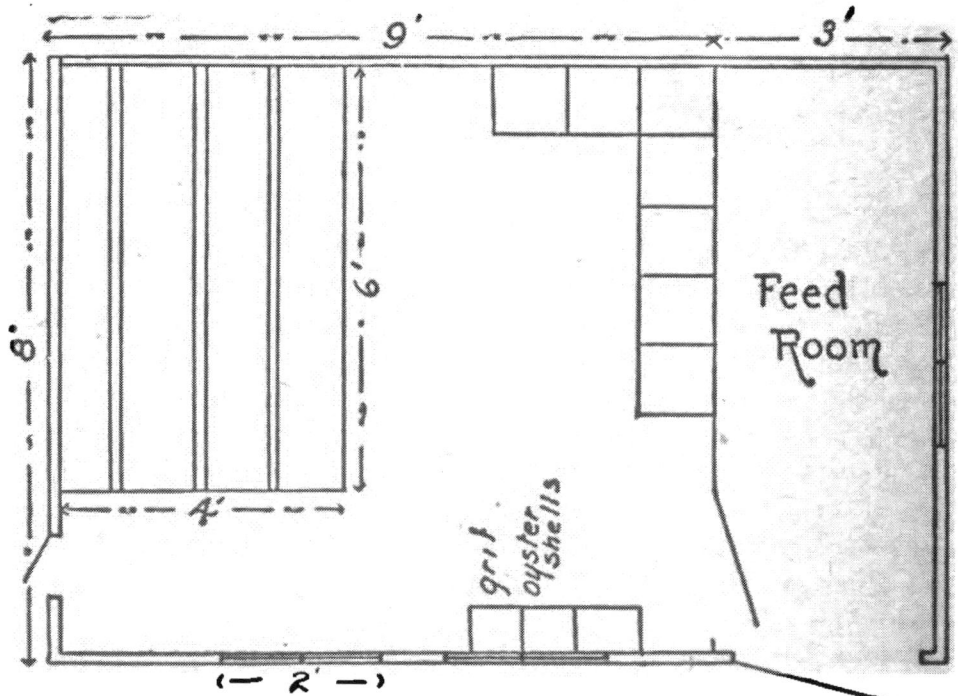

Illustration Showing the Location of Roosts, Nests, etc., in "A Ten Dollar Colony House."

Illustration of "A Ten Dollar Colony House."

It is the simplest kind of a house to build as will be seen by reference to the illustrations. The frame is made of 2 x 4s and is covered with common boards, planed on one side. The cracks are closed with battens on sides and roof. The house has a floor. I like a floor because it can be cleaned off easily and it is always dry. Using the droppings board is much better than letting the droppings fall on the floor I think. Every day I scrape the droppings in a box and remove them and every week I paint the roosts and spray the platform with liquid lice killer.

The building is lined with tar paper. It was put up cheaply, but it makes a nice comfortable house for a flock of fowls. I find the feed room in it very convenient. I keep all the feed there and I go there to mix and get it ready for feeding. A litter of clover hay about a foot deep is always on the floor, and I throw the grain in this litter and make the fowls scratch for it.

HOUSE FOR A BREEDING PEN.

A Compactly Arranged, Practical House for Eight to Ten Fowls.

By Harrison Bennett, Illinois.

This house is designed for a breeding pen of six or eight hens and a male. It is 8 feet long and 6 feet wide, 6 feet high in front and 4 feet high at the rear. The building is covered with tongued and grooved boards. The roof may be covered with roofing fabric or shingles as the builder prefers. A gravel or sand floor filled in to a height of several inches above the surface of the ground around the building will prove satisfactory.

I can explain the construction best by referring to the

Drawing, Showing the Construction of "House for a Breeding Pen," Designed by Harrison Bennett.

illustration. At the bottom of the front side, the hinged doors, AA, are made to swing outward and may be used for ventilators and as a place of exit for the fowls. There are two full windows in the front side, the upper sash of each, BB, being hinged at the top to permit additional ventilation. The shell, grit and charcoal box is represented by C and the drinking fountain by I. The ventilator shaft, D, enters through the roof and extends nearly to the floor and is used chiefly in cold weather when the windows cannot be opened. There is also an exit for impure air in the front corner. It is a shaft which opens near the roof on the inside and extends to the floor, with a hole through the side of the building near its base to allow the air to pass out. A canvas (cotton cloth or burlap would be better—Ed.) curtain, E, may be let down in front of the roost during cold weather to form a cozy roosting place.

The roosts, FF, are two in number, placed 1 foot apart. The droppings board, G, is 2 feet 6 inches by 6 feet and the nest boxes, HHHH, are placed beneath this platform. The nests and droppings board are built so that they may be removed from the building for convenience when cleaning the house.

A TWO PEN COLONY HOUSE.

A Poultry Building for Two Flocks of Fowls that Can Be Constructed for Forty Dollars.

By C. A. Pfeiffer, Minnesota.

The accompanying illustrations show one of our individual colony houses built in the orchard. We call it a combination house, for we use it for indoor brooders early in

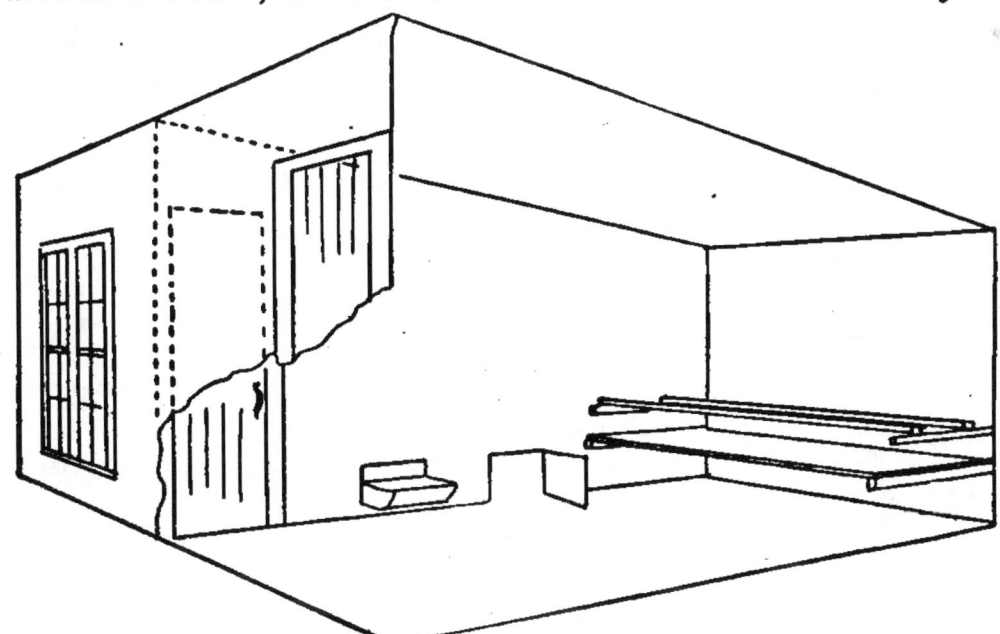

Illustration Showing the Manner of Building C. A. Pfeiffer's Colony House.

the spring, later for a colony house and in the winter for surplus stock or breeding pens.

This house is 10 x 16 feet in size, divided into two equal sized rooms by a solid partition with a large door and trap door, each room being 8 x 10 feet. The house faces the south. The roosting room is on the east side, scratching room on west side; either, or both sides can be used for brooders.

In building this house we used good heavy sills, resting on stone footings. Studding and rafters are 2 x 4 inches,

Two of C. A. Pfeiffer's Colony Houses in Use on Mr. Pfeiffer's Plant.

and the building is sheeted with fence flooring all around. The roof is covered with No. 2 and the sides with No. 1, prepared roofing of a well-known brand, making it air and water tight. The floors are of cinders which are filled in to the top of sills and covered with sand, so the surface is always dry.

We used a lot of old material in building this house and therefore cannot state definitely what one would cost when all the material had to be purchased and labor hired, but figuring on the cost of such material as we had to purchase, we think it would cost $40.00 for each house.

COLONY HOUSE FOR A CITY LOT.

A Plan for Roosting Room, Scratching Room, Store Room and Root Cellar Under One Roof.

By Mrs. Geo. M. Ray, Minnesota.

This house is designed for a city lot where a flock of twenty-five fowls is kept. It has in view the complete equipment of such a house, permanency, and the demand for sanitary conditions and attractive appearance.

The house is 20 feet long, 12 feet wide, 6 feet high at the eaves and 8 feet in the center, with a roof sloping both ways, the gables east and west, and the house facing south. It is divided into three compartments. The first, in the west end and nearest the dwelling house, is 7 x 12 feet, a food and scratching room; the second, 9 x 12 feet, the roosting room; the third, 4 x 12, is a room where tools, brood coops and the barrels for dust and droppings are kept.

A brick or stone foundation, 2 feet deep, is built, with a cross wall 7 feet from the west end, separating the floor of the scratching room from the rest of the building. To make it rat proof the outside wall is extended outward at the bottom the length of one brick and the depth of two. Between the cross wall and the east end wall a slight excavation is made, the depth of which is increased to several feet under the middle room to provide a place to store several bushels of beets and turnips and to hang from the joists, roots upward, a supply of cabbage for the winter.

The sills are 4 x 6, the cross floor timbers, 2 x 4, laid 2 feet apart, except in the scratching room where there is no floor but earth. The studding, 2 x 4, is placed about three feet apart, but varies to accommodate the partitions on the north side, and windows and doors elsewhere. The rafters, 2 x 4, are two feet apart. Sides, ends and roof are covered with heavy paper and boarded. Good shin-

26   POULTRY HOUSES.

gles are used on the roof and good siding in all the walls and partitions.

The partitions are built up to the height of the eaves, one on the brick cross wall, the other four feet from the east end. A double action, self-closing door is placed in each partition near the south side. The floor is double with paper between. A trap door enters the root cellar from the middle room. Boards are laid loose on top of the partitions to form a loft for clover and for the straw needed for the floors, which, packed in closely, adds to the warmth

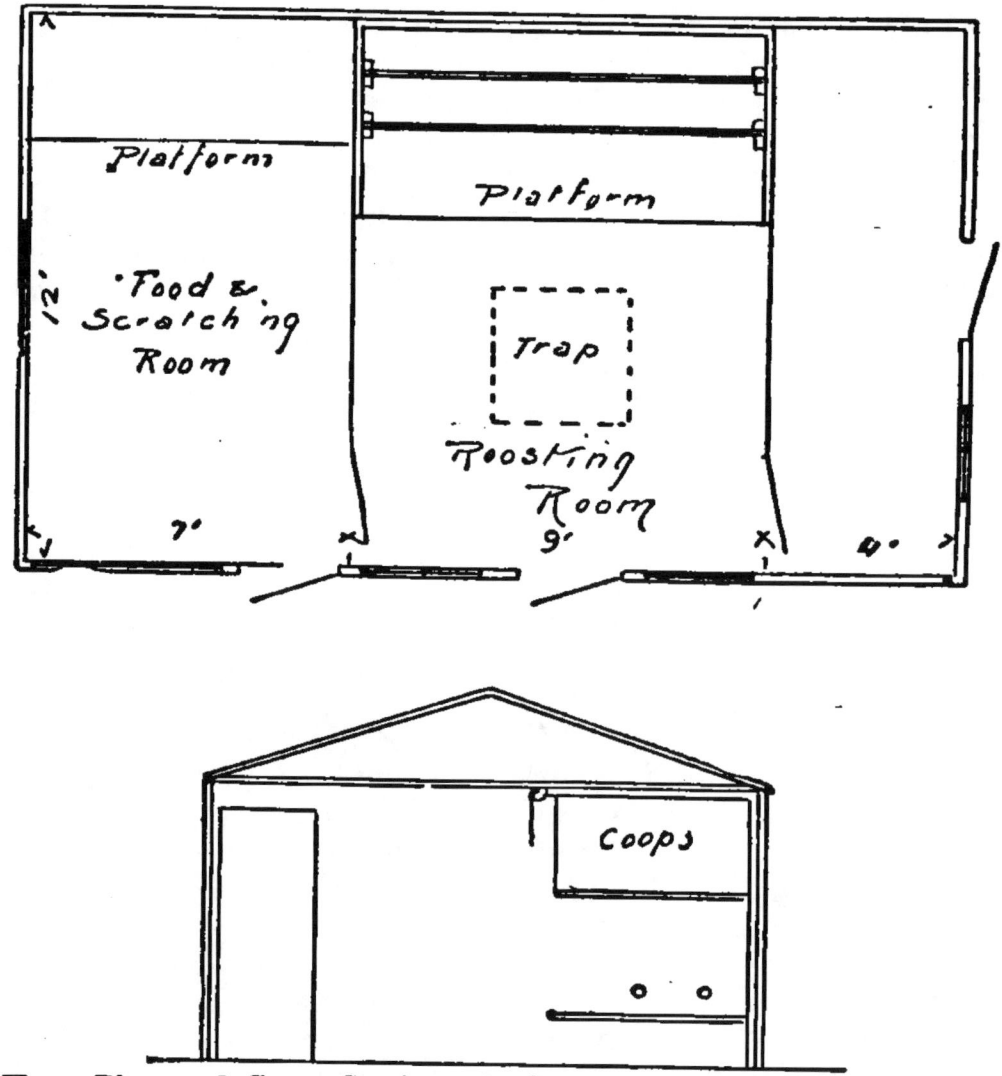

Floor Plan and Cross Section of "Colony House for a City Lot," Designed by Mrs. Ray, Showing the Arrangement of Pens and the Location of Fixed and Movable Equipment.

of the house. Two pieces of 2 x 4 with cross pieces nailed on every ten inches makes a good ladder by which to reach the loft.

An outside door 3 feet wide is made in the east wall of the tool house and a window beside it to the south. Shelves and hooks are placed where most convenient. In the south wall of the roosting room are two glass windows, 2½ feet wide and there is a door 3 feet wide, consisting of a frame covered with muslin, between them. In the scratching room a door 3 feet wide hinged close to the partition opens outward. In the remaining space there is a cloth covered window space, 4 x 4 feet. In the center of the west end there is a window with a glass filled sash in winter and a

Exterior View of "Colony House for a City Lot," Designed by Mrs. Ray.

mosquito wire covered frame in summer, built near the ground and made to swing as a door.

Across the north side of the scratching room a loose platform is built, 3 feet wide, for three barrels to hold the grain. Small sacks of other kinds of grain are suspended from hooks and nails above and a shelf ten inches wide runs around this space a foot from the top on which is kept the brush broom for cleaning the open drinking vessels, a knife, scissors, twine, markers, lice powder, lime and such things. When a rat proof foundation is not built this food closet should be entirely inclosed with fine mesh wire. Where food is always standing open rats will gather and many little chickens are sure to be a part of their diet.

Boxes for grit and other things constantly required are placed low on the walls of the pens.

The north side of the roosting room is lined with flooring on the inside of the studding and the space filled with fine sawdust, packed tight. The sides of this roosting compartment extend out into the room four feet. The ceiling is made on a level with the top of the partition, with a 2 x 4 piece of lumber 4 feet from the back, to meet the verticle edges of the sides. Boards are nailed on this cross piece above and below and the space filled with sawdust, packed. A platform, 4 feet wide, is built across this compartment fifteen inches from the floor and two movable perches are placed six inches above it. The first one is ten inches from the rear wall, the second one twelve inches nearer the front edge.

Two and a half feet above the platform and one foot nine inches from the ceiling there is a shelf the same size as the platform. It is divided into two coops and slatted in front, with a door in each division. This is for hens, broody or a little of out condition. A muslin curtain is hung from the ceiling to be let down in front of coops and roosts at night in cold weather.

Trap nests are placed in the middle room, on the floor under the roost, or open nests are hung on the wall with a very sloping muslin or wire screen covering them, to prevent the hens from sitting on the edges. The openings are in front with an alighting board running their entire length. Narrow platforms on brackets are put in the most sheltered place in this room for the water fountains, usually on the east wall near the roosts.

The primary use of these rooms has been named. They are so arranged that when hatching time arrives the hens may be confined to the middle room and its yard and the end rooms may be used for the needs of the brooding season. The scratching room is used for a hatching room and the tool room accommodates unruly sitters or extra hens with broods. After the chickens are weaned they are returned to the scratching room and yard to remain there until transferred into their winter quarters.

COLONY HOUSE WITH PROTECTED ROOSTS.

A Drop Curtain Protects the Fowls on the Roosts During Cold Winter Nights.

By G. E. Longeway, Montana.

It is desirable to build this house with a southern exposure where the ground slopes away from the house, insuring dry floors and a clean yard. Both the sills and the plates of this house should be 4 x 6 inches in size and framed at the corners. The building should be boarded up and down with boards of uniform width. The sides should be double boarded with the best building paper between, two thicknesses on the corners and one thickness elsewhere. For rafters use 2 x 4 pieces, set 2 feet apart. The roof should be single boarded with the same material that is used on the sides, then covered with the same grade of building paper and shingled, laying the shingles four inches to the weather. The window has a single sash, 3 x 6 feet, hinged on the sides like a door and

Colony House Designed by G. E. Longeway.

may be swung back against the inside wall. On the inside of the sash tack fine mesh wire netting and on the outside coarse mesh netting. The window is held closed by a spring catch and fastened open with a hook. The door is 2 feet wide and 6 feet high, made of inch boards, with

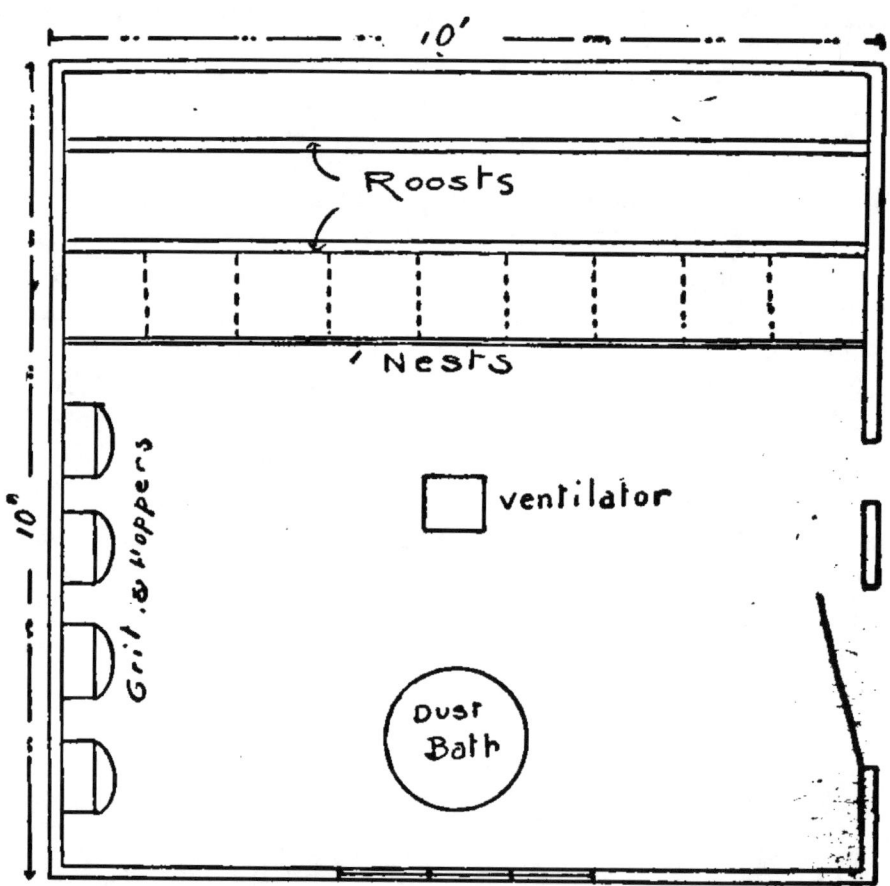

Plan of Colony House Designed by G. E. Longeway, Showing Arrangement of Equipment.

paper between, all properly cased, fitted and hung, having a lock and a hook to hold it closed and one to hold it open. In one end of the building about a foot from the door and toward the roost, cut a hole 8 x 12 inches for a chicken door and fit it with a small drop door which should be supplied with a hook to hold it closed and another to hold it open.

The ventilator should be made of 1 x 10 inch boards, four being nailed together to form a box or shaft. This should reach from a point about 18 inches above the floor,

COOPS AND EQUIPMENT.

in the center of the house, to the roof and thence to the front of the house and out through the wall just under the eaves. Allow this box to project 10 inches outside the wall, nail a board over the end and cut an opening in the underside for an exit for the air. Put a sliding board in this ventilator box about 3 feet above the floor to serve as a

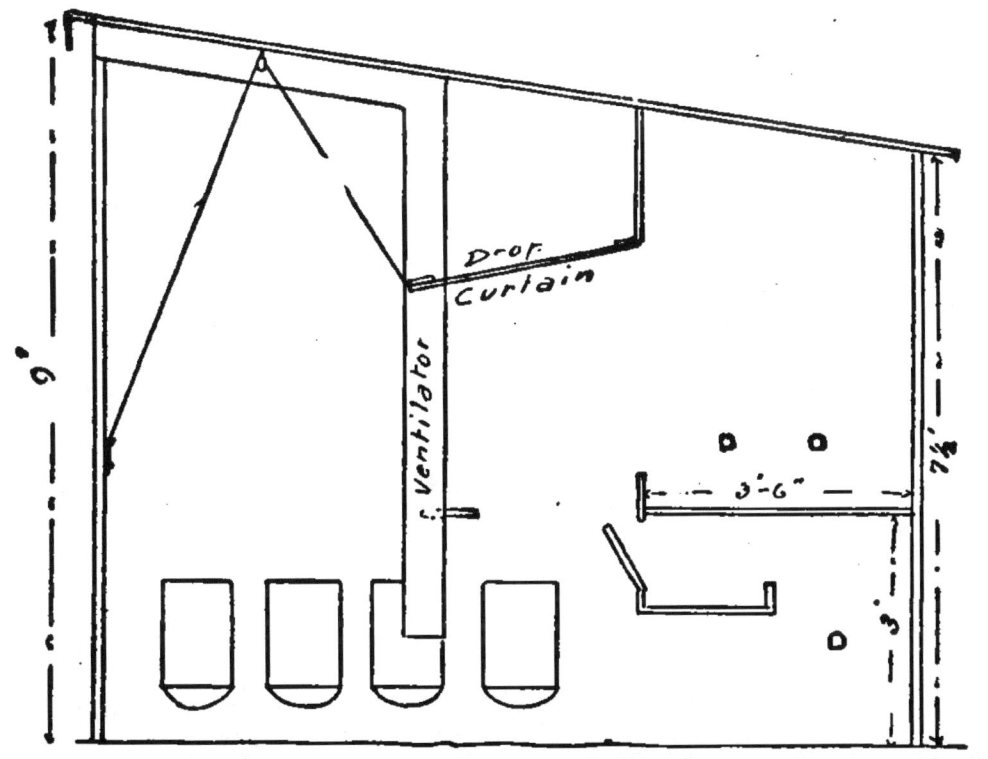

Cross Section of Colony House Designed by G. E. Longeway, Showing Position of Ventilator and Protected Roosts.

damper and tack a piece of coarse mesh muslin over the end of the shaft that is within the house.

The droppings board should be 3 feet above the floor, 3 feet 6 inches wide and made of inch matched lumber. Two full length roosts are placed 8 inches above the droppings board and 15 inches apart. The roosts may be of 2 x 3-inch stuff with the corners rounded and should be made removable. The nests, which are located under the droppings board, are 12 inches wide, 14 inches high and 15 inches deep. They are made of inch lumber and are closed in front by a hinged door. At the rear of the nests is placed a board 15 inches from the floor for the hens to fly upon when entering them.

The inside of the walls of the house and the inside of the roof over the roosts should be covered with building paper firmly tacked on. A drop curtain should be made of heavy muslin or burlap and tacked to the under side of the roof directly over the front edge of the droppings board. It should be long enough to reach a few inches below the edges of the board. To draw the curtain up and out of the way when not needed, fasten to the lower edge a 2-inch strip

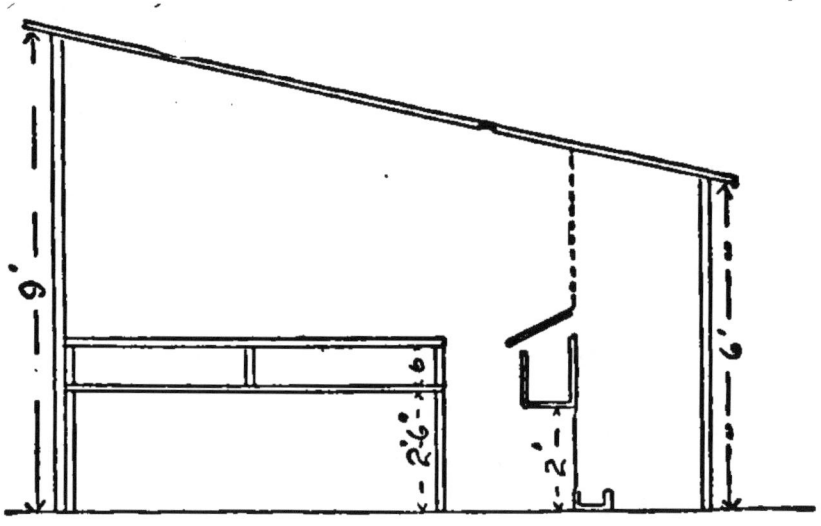

Cross Section of Louis Riedesel's Colony House.

of board and to this, at each end, fasten small ropes which pass through pulleys fastened to the ceiling 4 feet in front of the edge of the droppings board. In this way the curtain can be drawn up and fastened out of the way.

The floor of the house may be of sand or of cinders as preferred. The entire inside of the house should be whitewashed. Place half of a barrel in front of the window and fill it two thirds full with road dust and wood ashes for a dust bath. Place grit boxes on the wall opposite the door, also hoppers for dry feed. In building this house use whatever lumber is cheapest in your part of the country.

A CONVENIENT POULTRY HOUSE.

A Plan for Building a Colony House With a Labor Saving Arrangement of Interior Fixtures.

By Louis Riedesel, North Dakota.

This poultry house is 12 x 16 feet on the ground, 9 feet high in front and 6 feet high in the rear. It has three windows, two on the south side and one on the east end

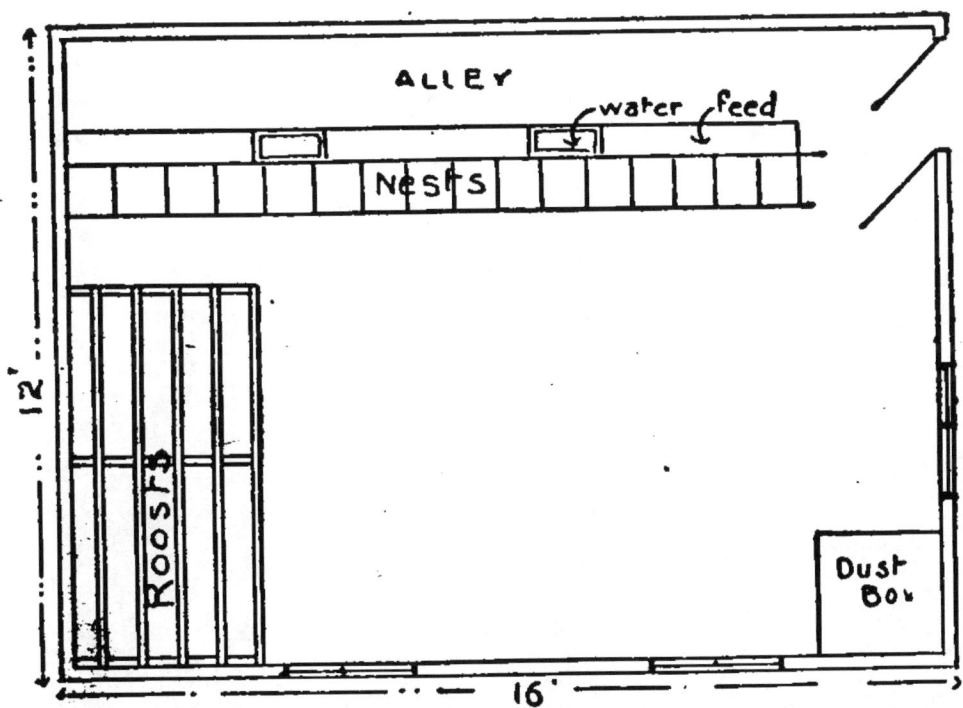

Drawing Showing the Arrangement of Fixtures in Louis Riedesel's Colony House.

which admit plenty of sunlight. There are no windows on the north and west, thus making a warm corner for roosts and avoiding draughts. It is covered with shiplap. paper and siding on the outside, is ceiled on the inside and has a good shingle roof.

Before the floor is laid, the ground beneath should be dug out and sand put in to fill the space to the height of 4 inches above the ground outside which protects the floor from dampness. A raised platform is built 2½ feet from the main floor in one end of the house (see illustration,) six inches above which are the roosts. The roosts rest upon a frame fastened to the wall with hinges so that it can be easily raised and the platform cleaned in a very short time each morning.

The alley is separated from the pen by wire netting, except under the nests, where vertical slats should be used, placed 2 inches apart. Between these slats the chickens feed out of a trough that sits in the alley, where they cannot get into it with their feet.

The nests are made along the alley, 2 feet from the floor, with an incline roof so the chickens cannot roost on them. Eggs can be gathered from the alley through openings in the side near the tops of the nests; the hens enter the nests from the pen.

(It will be noted on referring to the plan that the attendant enters this house through a door in the Northeast corner and enters the pen through a door at the left, in the partition. Though most poultrymen do not believe that a walk is necessary in a house for one flock, so much of the labor of caring for the birds may be performed without entering the pen that the use of space for this purpose in this plan seems justified.—Editor)

View of Louis Riedesel's Colony House When Completed.

CONTINUOUS HOUSES

A SCRATCHING SHED HOUSE.

A Building with Open Front Scratching Sheds and Curtain Front Roosting Pens Proves Healthful for the Fowls.

By Fred A. Mallery, Minnesota.

This house is covered with dressed and matched fencing, 4 feet long, which was the cheapest lumber I could buy. The roof is covered with three-ply roofing paper. The roosting pens are double boarded all around and lined with tar felt. The partition between pens is single boarded, but solid, and the scratching pens are single boarded all around. There is no glass in this house; the windows have curtains on swinging frames that go up against the front of house, the inside, in the daytime. There were only 5 days last winter (1905-6) that the curtains were down all day. Each scratching pen has an open front and no curtain; the house faces the south and is protected on the west so that no curtain is needed.

I did not have a sick chicken or a frosted comb last winter and I could not ask them to lay any better. When it was eighteen degrees below outside, it was just thirty-two degrees above on a post two feet in front of the roosts. There is room for fifty-five Plymouth Rocks in each pen. The hole for hens to go from one pen to the other is under the droppings boards. These droppings boards are 2½ feet above the ground and 3 feet 9 inches wide, boarded crosswise, with the two center boards one foot longer to make a place on which to set the water dish in the winter, where it will always be clean. The ground floor is always

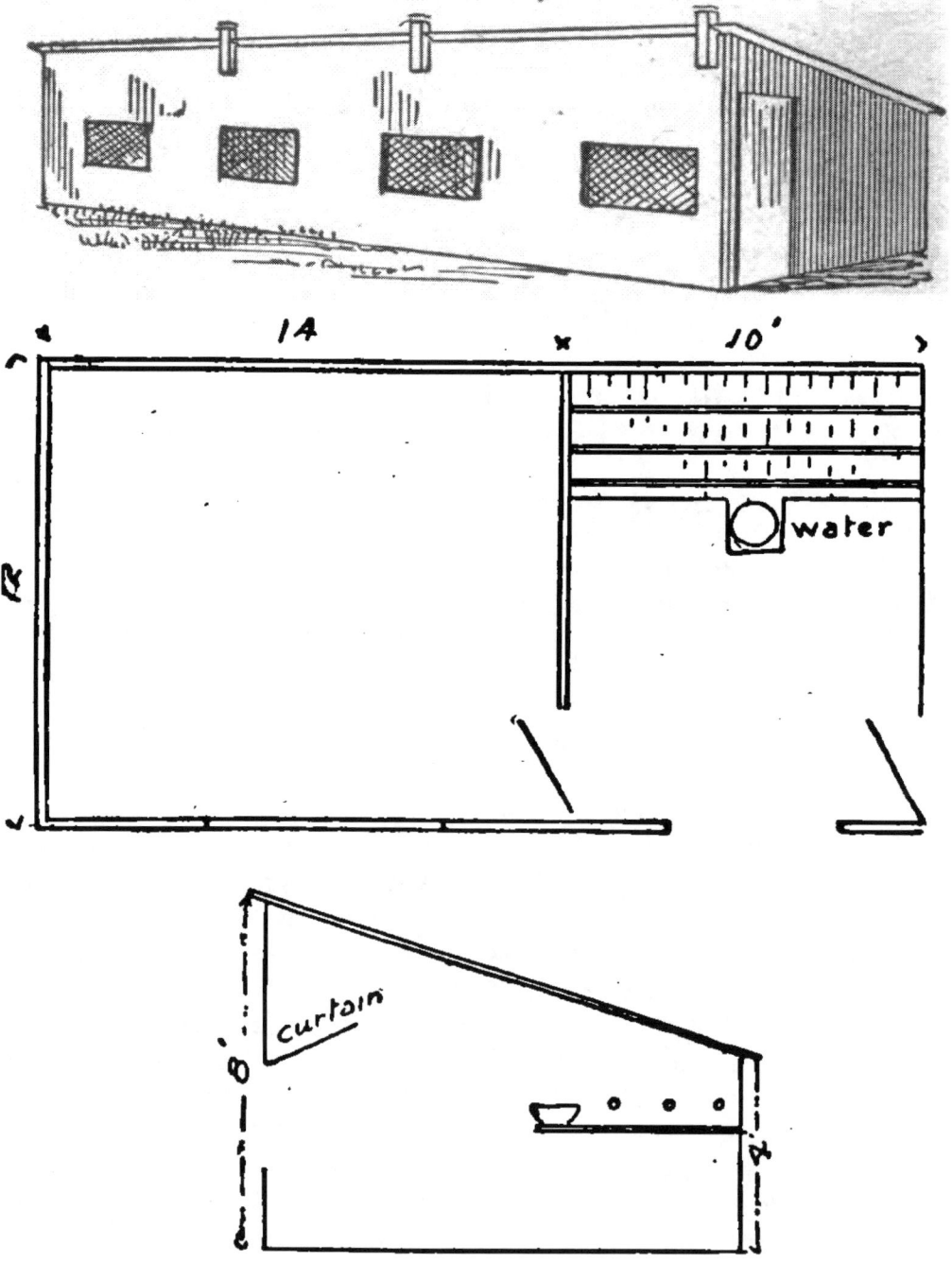

Illustration of the Exterior, Floor Plan and Cross Section of "A Scratching Shed House," Designed by Fred A. Mallery.

dry and the roosting room is just as dry in winter as it is in summer. I could and did scratch matches on the boards over the chickens' heads when it was below zero outside. I had dust boxes, but the hens did not use them. One scratching pen is two feet longer than the other and I put in a wire partition to make a place for sitting hens and feed.

This is not a house on paper, but one that has been in use two years. I formerly used glass windows and had a damp house; last winter I took out the glass and tacked common muslin on the frames. This house is open to visitors at any time. I feed dry mash in hoppers with grain in clover hay scratching litter.

(Nothing is said of the dimensions of this house in this description, but each roosting pen and its adjacent scratching shed should afford not less than 300 square feet of floor space if it is to accommodate fifty-five fowls.—Editor.)

RAT PROOF POULTRY HOUSE.

A Building Lined with Wire Netting Prevents All Danger from Rodents.

By Louis Riedesel, North Dakota.

This house covers a space 16 x 48 feet and can be built as long as desired. Its 4 x 6 sills are set on the ground and 2 x 4 plates are used. It is boarded up and down with 12-inch boards. The windows, each with nine lights of 10 x 14 glass, are fastened with hinges at the top, to swing out. The inside of the frame is covered with inch mesh wire netting, and on the sills I use inch mesh wire 24 inches wide extending down into the ground outside one foot to keep out rats and skunks. The floor is of gravel.

Each pen is 8 x 11 feet and supposed to hold twelve to fifteen fowls. The nest boxes are 6 feet long and 18 inches wide with holes in front large enough to reach in and take out the eggs. The boxes are placed one foot from the back partition and open at one end so the hens can get in behind them and are loose so they can be turned over

38 POULTRY HOUSES,

and cleaned out and sprayed. The droppings boards are 3 inches above the nest boxes and are fastened to the partition next to the walk with hinges so they may be turned up against the partition. The roosts are two pieces

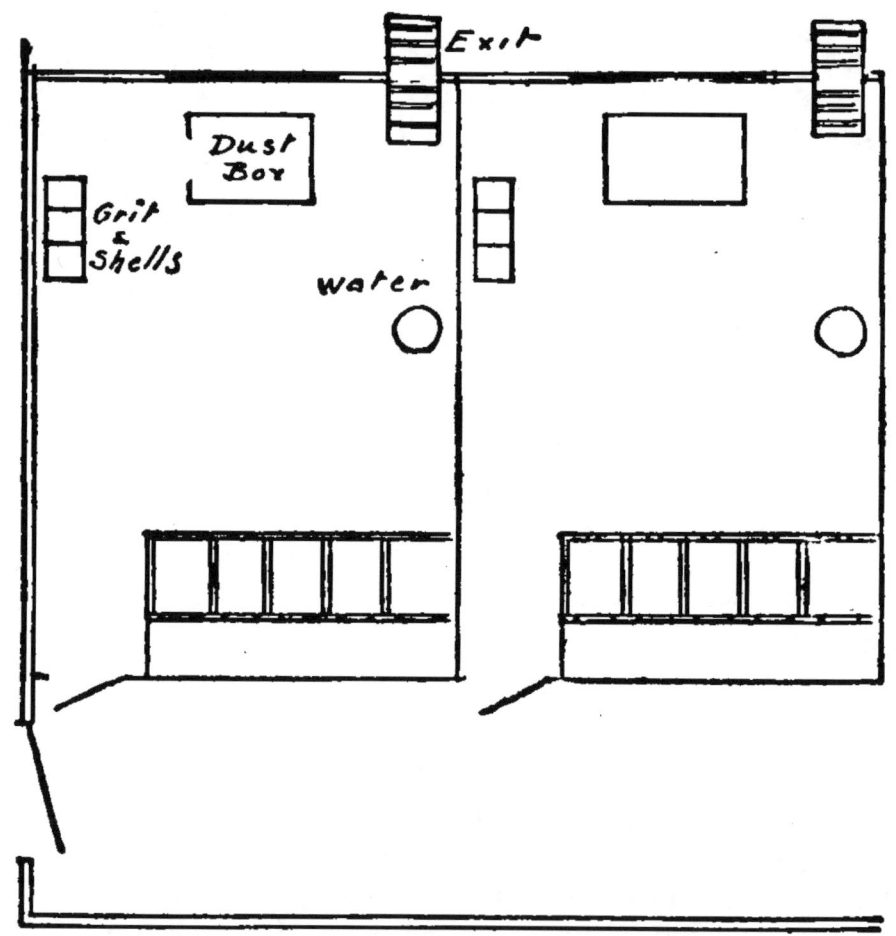

Floor Plan Showing Arrangement of the Interior Fixtures and Utensils in Louis Riedesel's Poultry House.

of 2 x 4, 6 feet long, rounded off on the edges to nearly one half round, fastened 14 inches apart with pieces of 2 x 4 spiked to their ends, which are also fastened to the partition with hinges. The partition is boarded 5 feet high with matched shiplap, then wire to the rafters. The partitions between the pens are boarded up 3 feet and filled with wire to the rafters. There are four ventilating flues in the roof.

COOPS AND EQUIPMENT.

In cold climates this house should be built with 2 x 4 studding, have matched lumber on the outside and be ceiled inside with matched lumber and either back plastered or lined with tar paper.

In the alley, leading into each pen, is a door 2 feet wide filled with wire netting, fastened with screen door hinges with springs to close the door behind one. In front of the windows are dust boxes 2 x 3 feet, right where the sun always strikes them. In this climate all that is required is that the house be boarded with straight edge boards and battened with 1 x 4 boards. Each pen has a three partition grit and shell box and a water fountain.

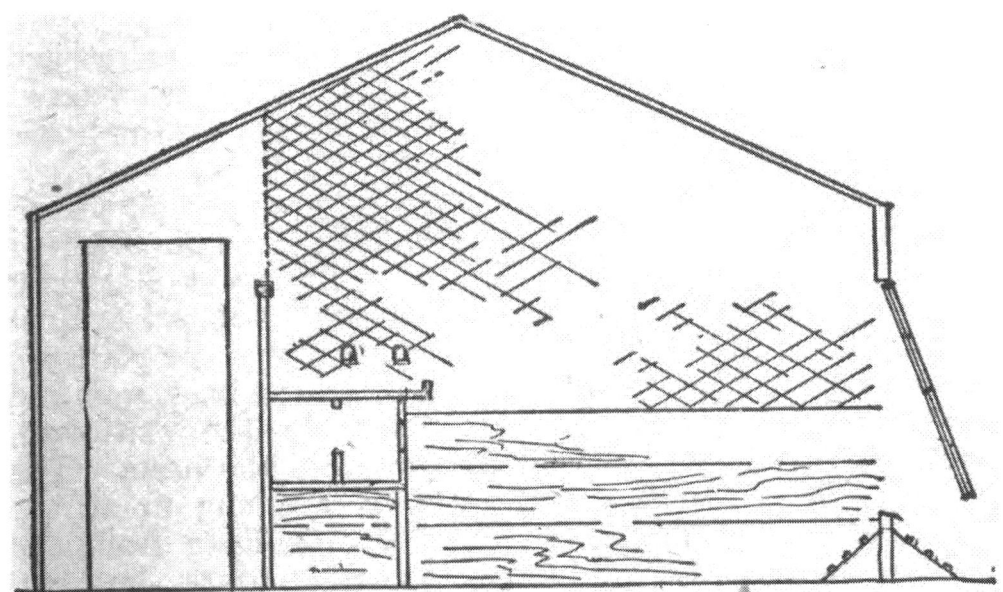

Cross Section Showing Partition, the Location of Roosts and Nests and the Manner of Hanging Window so That it May be Opened and Closed to Ventilate the House.

A SHED ROOF HOUSE.

The Designer of this Poultry House Recommends it as Simple and Inexpensive but Thoroughly Satisfactory.

By A. A. Ziemer, Minnesota.

This plan is for building a house 30 x 15 feet, 8 feet high in front and 6 feet high in the back. It is simply but well built of small dimension stuff and matched boards, covered on the outside with prepared roofing and lined with tar paper. It is a very light and warm house. Wire netting is stretched on the underside of the rafters and the space between it and the roof is stuffed with oat straw which keeps the house warm and free from dampness.

The house is divided into three sections by partitions of wire netting and each section, or pen, has two windows in front, each 24 x 28 inches in size. The roost platforms are 2 feet above the floor and 3 feet wide, placed against the back wall. The roosts are 12 inches above the platform and rest upon a frame which is hinged to the back wall and may be turned up to facilitate cleaning the platforms. Underneath the front of the platforms are the nests. The hens approach the nests from the rear, going in at the ends of the platforms and hinged boards hang from the fronts of the platforms to keep the nests dark, but can be raised when the attendant collects the eggs. The front of the platform is supported by a 2 x 4 piece at each corner and the back is fastened to the wall.

The positions of the dust baths, water cans, grit and shell boxes, etc., are indicated on the plan as are also the the positions of exterior and interior doors and doors for the fowls. The clover rack is made of 4-inch mesh wire netting and is 4 feet high and 2 feet in diameter. Its position in each pen is indicated on the ground plan. At the back of each pen is an opening in the wall 8 x 12 inches which is opened when the weather permits but closed at night, except in the hot months of summer. Muslin is tacked over these openings during the winter to prevent a draft when the wooden shutters are open. Over each outside door is an opening 8 x 14 inches which is open nearly all the time, winter and summer, but which is covered with muslin in winter. During cold winter nights a muslin curtain is let down in front of the roosts and also over the windows.

Everything considered, this is a practical, satisfactory and inexpensive building and one which will give everyone thorough satisfaction.

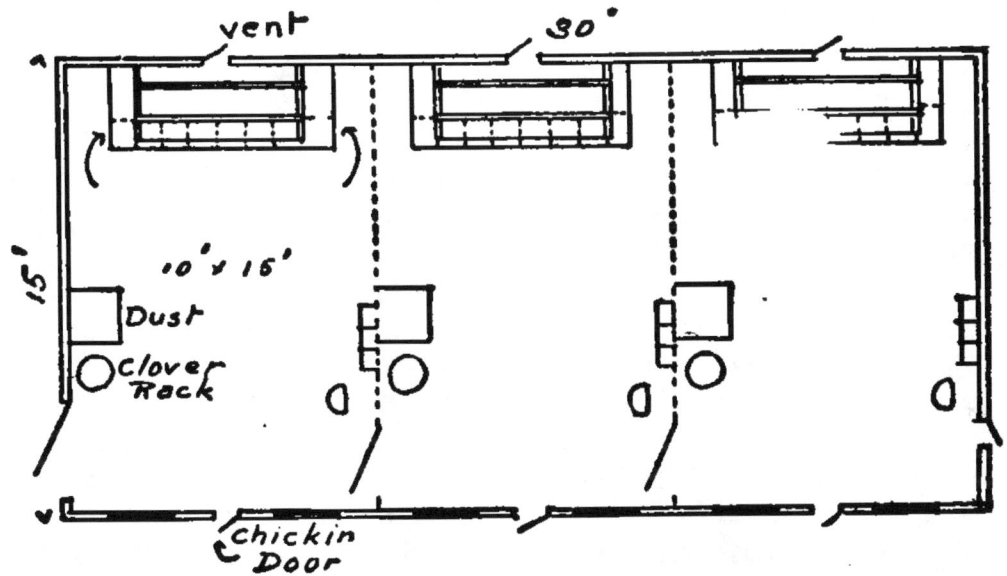

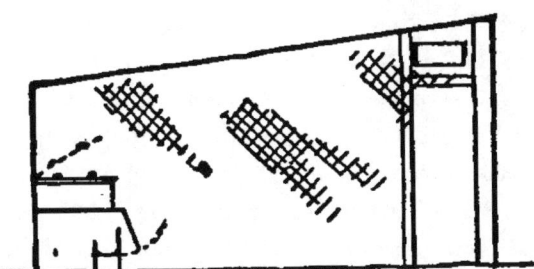

Ground Plan and Cross Section, Showing the Location of Partitions, Roosts and Roost Platforms, Ventilators and Other Fixtures and Utensils in the Poultry House Designed by A. A. Ziemer.

A CURTAIN FRONT HOUSE.

A Continuous Poultry House that Has No Glass in the Windows, but is Provided with Muslin Curtains and Proves Satisfactory in Minnesota.

By C. E. Boddy, Minnesota.

It is of the utmost importance that the poultry house be built right. In one sense it is the foundation of the business. If it is well adapted to the purpose it tends to keep up a poultryman's interest in his fowls. If the building is not right, the results are not what they should be and the poultryman gets discouraged and further neglects his flock. We see too many plans of poultry houses given in the journals that are generally the result of someone's first experience. Many times these plans are not practical, are too expensive, and altogether unsuitable. The plan I give here is the result of much experience with different styles of houses. While I make no claim to originality for this house I have never seen one like it.

The foundation should be of stone, brick or grout, and extend 18 inches below the surface of the ground to prevent heaving by frost and to exclude rats. The sills should be 4 x 4 inches. I prefer a good board floor to anything else. A board floor covered half an inch deep with sand or gravel, with several inches of litter on top, is easy to keep clean.

This building may be double boarded with tar paper between, or have one thickness of cheap boards placed up and down covered outside with tar paper. In this locality shingles make the best and cheapest roof. The rafters are of 2 x 4 scantling placed two feet apart. In a shed roof it would be necessary to use 2 x 6 rafters to prevent sagging.

I do not believe anything is gained by going to too great expense in trying to make a warm building unless it is intended to use artificial heat. I have a building boarded, papered, back plastered and plastered on the face of the studs and lined inside with building paper, but I cannot see that it is much warmer than the boarded and papered building and it is much harder to keep dry. In this plan the roosts are not against the cold north wall and it is not necessary to make this wall as expensive as if the roosts were placed directly against it.

An alley in a poultry house has been objected to as a

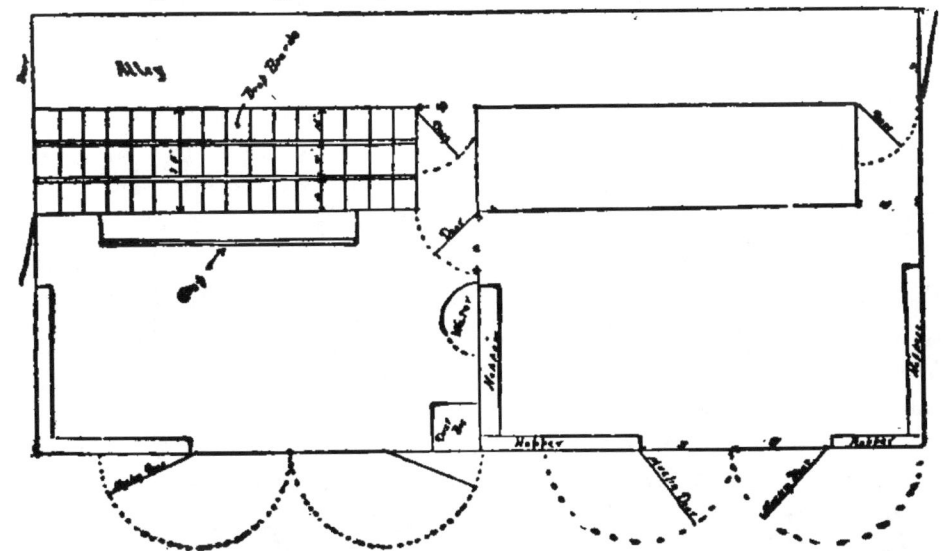

Illustration Showing the Arrangement of Interior Fixtures and Manner of Hanging the Curtains which Serve as Windows in "The Curtain Front House" Designed by C. E. Boddy.

useless waste of room, besides making more work going from one room to another when feeding. We have overcome this objection by placing a door in each partition leading directly from one room to the next. Without an alley the droppings must be carried through each pen or in and out of each pen. It is the same when gathering eggs. Eggs should be gathered several times a day in winter to prevent chilling, and also at other times to prevent hens acquiring the egg eating habit. An alley is worth all it costs for the purpose of gathering eggs alone when the nests can be reached from it without entering the pens. With a hoe having a handle about two feet long, and a blade bent at right angles to the handle, and a wheel-barrow with a box that comes under the projection of the droppings boards, it is a simple matter to go along the alley and clean the droppings boards. The muslin covered frames back of droppings boards are very simple affairs and require nothing but the button at the top to hold them in place. This arrangement is better than hinges. In a house without an alley the nests are usually placed under the droppings boards, thus taking up as much floor space as does the alley. Besides, this makes dark corners in which hens will lay, and it is no pleasant task to crawl under there after eggs. In the plan given here the hens have use of all the floor space. The water vessel and grit and feed hoppers can be arranged as desired. They could be placed under the nests and filled from alley, but hens always scratch litter away from light so I have shown them here placed against other walls. The wire netting panels in the front of the house should be on hinges and open inside, affording access to the yard. I prefer to have the muslin frames open outward, as they can be opened and closed more quickly than by entering each pen, and without disturbing the fowls.

It will be noticed that there is no glass in this house. Glass is covered with frost in cold weather, unless it is double, so that it does not admit any sunshine and it makes the house colder at night. It is hard to make one who has never tried it believe that these curtain front houses are warm enough and that they require no windows of glass. I have never seen a day so cloudy and dark that it was not light enough behind these closed curtains. There are very few days when it is necessary to close these muslin doors and very few nights that it is necessary to lower the curtains before the roosts. My flock of Barred Plymouth Rocks are in a muslin front house without windows. There was not a night the past winter that the curtains were down in front of the roosts and a healthier, more vigorous flock would be hard to find. The muslin used is the common, unbleached kind that sells for six or eight cents a yard. It is not burlap. It should not be stretched tightly and should not be oiled. It will last several years. The muslin covered openings in the front of the house can be made larger if desired or a small glass window can be put in each pen.

My hens never frost their combs in this house but with

COOPS AND EQUIPMENT. 45

the larger comb varieties it would be unecessary to be more careful about using curtains.

In the plan I have shown a step in front of droppings board as my heavy hens cannot fly to a perch 2 feet, 8 inches high. This step would not be necessary for lighter breeds. Good, strong strips of 2-inch furring, flat side up, are strong enough for perches if supports are used every six feet. The space at both ends of the perches is boarded with thin lumber and the space overhead filled with straw as shown in the plan.

All inside doors are hung on spring hinges such as are

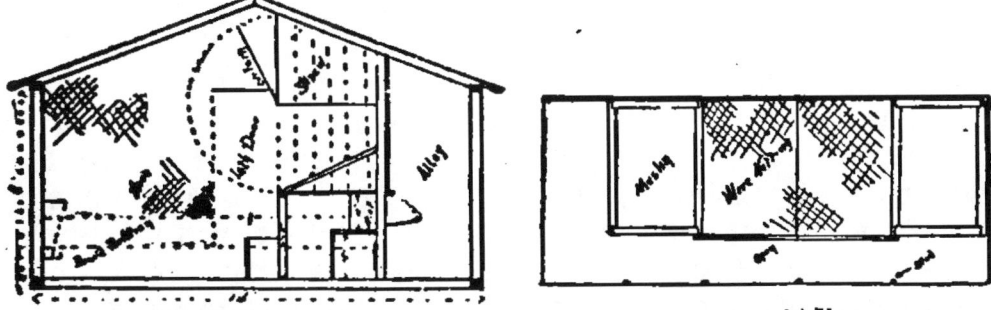

The Illustration at the Left Shows the Arrangement of Roosts and Nests and the Curtains which Protect the Fowls at Night; the Drawing at the Right Shows the Cloth Windows Open in Front of one of the Pens in the "Curtain Front House." Designed by C. E. Boddy.

used on screen doors. These hinges are inexpensive, and remove all danger of fowls from different pens getting mixed. These doors are hung one foot above the floor, the lower board of the partitioning continuing under each door. The door should be made tight a foot from the bottom to prevent the birds from fighting through. The partitions should be made tight to the height of 2 feet. Wire netting, muslin or lath may be used above this. The pens are 11 x 14 feet and each will accommodate about thirty fowls. Should it be desired to keep more than this number of hens in one pen the building may be made sixteen feet wide and pens twenty feet long. This would make pens 13 x 20 feet and would do for forty or fifty hens. In a long house, a shed for storing straw, built on the north side of the house and opening into the alley, is a convenience.

CONTINUOUS HOUSE WITH RAISED ALLEY.

Plan of Building Designed to "Keep the Cold Out" and Secure the Most Comfort to the Fowls and Greatest Convenience to the Owner.

By M. F. Stellwagen & Son, Minnesota.

We have bred poultry for some thirty odd years and during that time it has been our misfortune, or good fortune, as the case may be, to be located in a very cold climate. Poultry keepers and breeders have advocated all kinds of ventilators to supply fresh air during the winter, and I have used some of them, but have come to the conclusion that all my efforts should be directed toward keeping the cold air out and the house scrupulously clean. Having a door at each end of the house it can be aired very quickly and very thoroughly, so we think that the house we now have is as near correct as can be for our wants. This house can be built in warm climates and single roofs, doors, windows and siding can be used if desired.

The building is 70 feet long, but can, of course, be built any length. The scratching shed is the most important part of the building. Beginning at the front of the scratching shed, it is 3½ feet high at the eave of the roof. Where it joins the main building it is 5 feet 2 inches high and it is 7½ feet wide. The entire front of the scratching shed is of glass. These windows are the regular storm sash and are all made double with a 4-inch air space between them. The sides, ends, and roof are all made double, ceiling being used on the inside. Tarred felt is tacked on between the rafters and studding and then the entire space of 4 inches is filled is with planer shavings, packed solid. Where these cannot be procured leave that space empty, for a dead air chamber. Then we tack tarred felt to the studding and nail the siding on, so we have two thicknesses of tarred felt, ceiling siding and planer shavings, and the same for the roof ex-

COOPS AND EQUIPMENT. 47

cepting that we use a popular brand of prepared roofing on top of the roof boards, which are always matched flooring so that we get a good smooth surface for the roofing felt. With the outside walls and roof built in this way, we have a frost proof house, the poultry is kept comfortable and we get a good supply of eggs all winter. You

Photograph of "Continuous House With Raised Alley," Used by M. F. Stellwagen & Son.

will notice that the front of the main building also has plenty of windows which, like those in front of the scratching shed, are all built double. These supply light and sunshine for the dust baths and rear of the building. The scratching shed is 7½ feet wide, the building 12 feet wide and it is 2 feet 4 inches above scratching shed to roof of main building which is 7 feet 6 inches high at the front and 5 feet 6 inches at rear, these being outside measurements. The doors are 3 feet 2 inches wide. The floor of the alley is raised a foot above the ground which gives room for the fowls to pass back and forth from the scratching sheds to the main building. We use double doors and the inner door swings in—the floor of the alley being laid low at the ends so that the inner door will swing and inch boards put underneath to divide the pens.

The scratching pen has a matched board floor and the

main building has an earth floor. The pens are made 6 feet to 8 feet wide and both sides of the alley are covered with netting. Each pen has a door into the scratching sheds. We also leave an 8-inch space at the top of the scratching pen on the inside so that the attendant can scatter seed or grain into the scratching pens without opening the doors. This alley floor is laid 16 inches wide into the pen, that is outside of the alley proper. This projection affords the fowls room to jump up to get to the feed troughs and water fountains. As will be noticed we allow a space of 4 inches

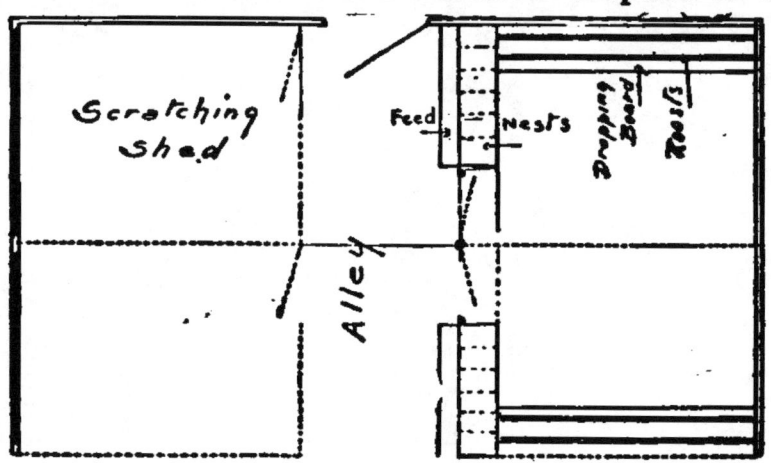

Floor Plan Showing the Location of the Alley and the Arrangement of Nests, Roosts, Roost Platforms, etc., in House Used by M. F. Stellwagen & Son.

above the floor of the alley so that the operator can pull the feed trough into the alley, fill it and push it back so that the fowls can eat, they standing on the 16-inch projection above spoken of. There is a feed trough and water dish for each pen. The attendant can feed and fill these water dishes (we use one gallon earthern milk crocks) from the alley. All feeding, egg collecting, in fact everything, except the cleaning of the droppings boards can be done from the alley.

You will notice that the droppings boards rest on the partitions of the pens. These droppings boards are of matched flooring and at the edges we have a 2 x 4 extending from end to end so that we do not need any posts to hold the ends of the droppings boards up.

Next comes the nests. These also open into the alley

and by having the openings for the hens away from the light and up above the roosts there is absolutely no danger of the hens getting into the habit of eating their eggs. We have never had one do that since we adopted these nests. Each pen has a door which swings into the pen and they are fitted so that they just pinch in tight enough so there is no danger of their opening, so no hook or catch is needed. Each pen has a dust bath made of sifted coal ashes and sifted earth and we find that the fowls use these baths nearly every day all winter.

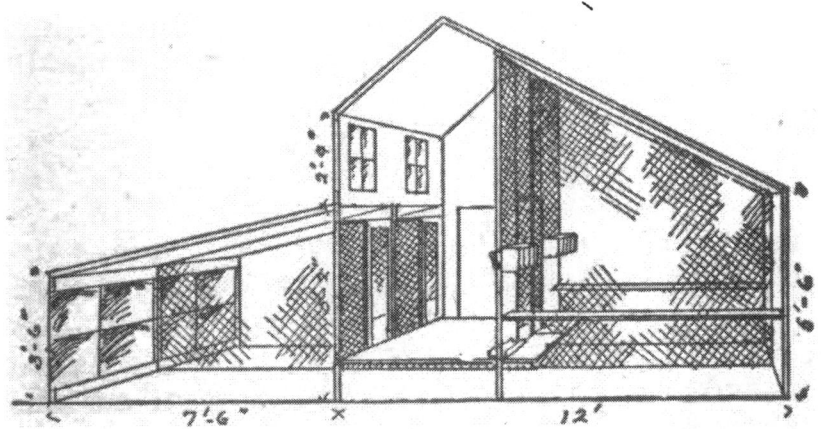

Illustration Showing the Manner of Constructing the House Used by M. F. Stellwagen & Son, Indicating the Position of Doors, etc.

This house can be built any length desired. The raised alleyway is the greatest convenience possible. The entire building is so convenient and compact that the work of taking care of the poultry is minimized, while not one foot of space is lost, and the fowls have plenty of sun in winter, or summer weather in January, and plenty of shade in summer. It is understood that we have doors 3 feet 2 inches wide at each end of the alleyway; these being made wide so the attendant can pass in and out with a wheel barrow. We have a poultry house in which the fowls will produce more winter eggs than any other we have ever tried, where the fowls are comfortable and happy, where there is no danger of egg eating and where the fowls can keep themselves free from vermin.

CONTINUOUS HOUSE WITH FEED ROOM.

Montana Poultry House With Curtain Front Scratching Shed and with Feed Room Connected.

By G. E. Longeway, Montana.

In building this poultry house in the most perfect manner a south or southeast exposure should be obtained, with the ground sloping in the same direction, thus making the house on higher ground than the yards; in this way all wash from the yards would be from the houses, insuring a dry house and scratching pen and a clean yard. The sills should be 4 x 6 inches, framed at the corners, with the plates 4 x 4 inches also framed at the corners. The boarding is up and down. The sides should be double boarded, care being taken to lap all cracks with the second boarding. Between the boards use the best grade of building paper, and around the corners of the house double the paper. For rafters use 2 x 4 pieces set 2 feet apart; the roof boards are the same as the siding. Cover the roof with the same grade of building paper and shingle, laying the shingles 4 inches to the weather.

The window in the roosting pen is a single sash, 3 x 6 feet, hinged on the side like a door and swings in and back against the inside wall. On the inside of the window frame tack fine mesh wire netting. On the outside of the window casing tack coarse mesh netting. The window is fastened with a spring catch and is held back by a hook. The door is 2 x 6 feet, made of inch boards, doubled, with tar paper between, all properly cased, fitted and hung, having lock and hook, and hook to hold it open. At the bottom of the door and in the center cut out a space 8 x 12 inches for a chicken door. Fit this with a drop board door, with a hook to hold it shut and a hook to hold it open. Make the chicken door between the house and scratching shed in the same way.

Inside of the house the ventilator should be made of boards 10 inches wide, four nailed together to form a box. This should reach from about 18 inches above the floor, in the center of the house, to the roof and thence to the

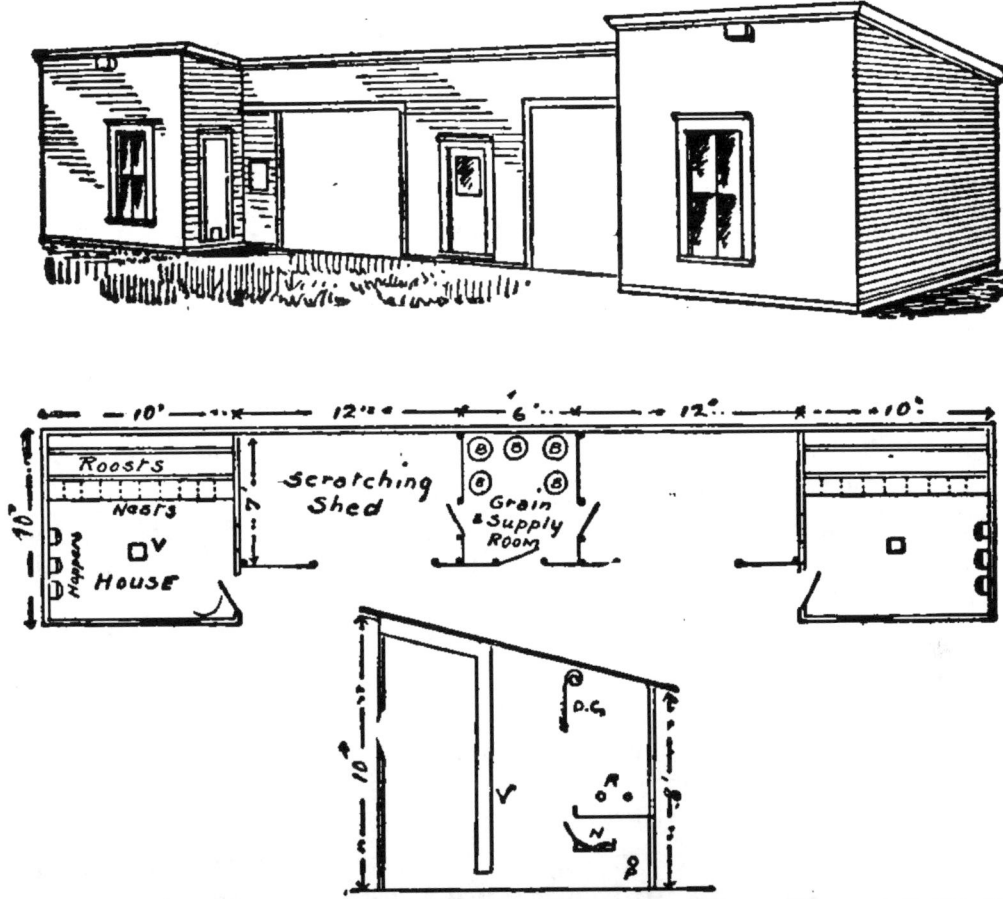

View of the Exterior and Drawing Showing Floor Plan and Cross Section of "Continuous House with Feed Room." Designed by G. E. Longeway.

front of the house and out through the wall. Allow the ventilator box to project outside ten inches and nail a board over the end, leaving the under side open for the air to get out. Put a sliding damper board in the box about 3 feet from the floor. Over the inside end of the ventilator, tack coarse mesh muslin. The droppings board should be 3 feet from the floor and 3 feet 6 inches wide, made of inch matched lumber. Two full length roosts, 2 x 3 inches with corners rounded, removable, are placed 8 inches above the droppings board and 15 inches apart. The nests are under the droppings board and 12 inches wide, 14 inches high and 15 inches deep, with the entrance for the hens from the rear. The front of the nests is closed by a hinged board door. Place a pole at the rear of the nests and 15 inches from the floor for the hens to fly on before entering the nests. The wall and roof back of and over the roosts is lined with building paper. A drop curtain made of heavy muslin or burlap is tacked to the underside of the roof exactly over the outer edge of the droppings board and is long enough to reach a few inches below the board. To draw the curtain out of the way, fasten to its lower edge a strip of board 2 inches wide and to this, close to each end, tie pieces of small rope, passing them through pulleys screwed in the roof 4 feet in front of droppings board. In this way the curtain can be pulled out of the way and fastened. The floor of the house may be of dirt or cinders, as preferred. The other fixtures in the house are grit boxes and hoppers for dry feed. These are fastened to the wall opposite the door. In front of the window is placed a half barrel, which is partly filled with road dust and wood ashes for a dust bath for the hens in winter.

The back wall and roof of the scratching shed are built exactly as those of the house, but the front of the shed is left nearly all open, only about two feet at each end being closed. These ends are single boarded with paper on the inside. In one end is fitted a small single sash window 15 x 20 inches. A burlap curtain is tacked to a frame fitted to the large opening in the front of the shed, hinged to the roof so it can be swung up inside and hooked to the roof.

The feed room is made like the house so far as outside walls and roof are concerned. The sides next the scratching sheds are single boarded and papered on the feed room side. The doors leading from the feed room to the sheds are of single boards papered on the inside and are 2 x 6 feet in size. The outside door is a panel door with double glass, cased and having latch and lock. Its size is 2 x 6 feet. The glass in this door is covered on the outside with fine mesh netting. All the doors into the feed room are fitted with springs to keep them closed. This feed room contains barrels enough to hold a year's supply of feed.

The interior of both houses and sheds should be whitewashed twice a year. The droppings boards should be covered with fine chaff or dirt every time they are cleaned. At least three inches of the ground floor should be removed each fall and fresh dirt supplied.

I have seen many so called model houses but to my mind and in my experience, this is the best for our northern climate. It has these features: First, it offers, light, warmth, good ventilation and comfort for the hens; second, it is easy to take care of; third, the expense of building it is not great.

A TIME SAVER.

Plan for Building a Continuous Poultry House in Which Most of the Work Can Be Done from the Walk.

By A. K. Johnson, North Dakota.

The poultry house illustrated herewith is 14 feet wide, 32 feet long and 8 feet high at the highest point, measured 4 feet in from the back wall. This forms a two-slant roof. The back wall is 6 feet high and the front is the same. It accommodates four breeding pens.

The hallway is 4 feet wide, making each pen 8 x 10 feet. There is a window containing twelve 8 x 10 lights in each pen. By glancing at the accompanying illustrations the manner of constructing this house will be plainly seen. The house is entered through a door in one end which opens into the hallway from which access to the pens is through doors each 2½ feet wide, framed of 3-inch boards and covered with 2-inch mesh wire netting. The nests rest upon platforms 2 feet wide, supported against the hallway partition on one side and by posts on the other, 18 inches from the floor. Above the nests and forming the top of the nest compartments are the droppings boards, 6 inches above which are the roosts. To facilitate gathering the eggs, removing the nests to clean them and cleaning the droppings board, two horizontal doors, hinged at the top, are placed one at the rear of the roosts and the other at

Exterior of Poultry House Designed by A. K. Johnson.

the rear of the nests, swinging out into the hallway. Under the nests is a lath partition through which the hens in the pens reach their heads into the hallway and secure the food from a trough, shown in the illustrations. This method of feeding the mash prevents the fowls soiling it by getting into it with their feet and also prevents undue crowding around the trough.

The hallway partition above the roosts is of 2-inch mesh wire netting. The partitions between the pens are boarded up 2 feet to prevent the fowls fighting through, above which the space to the roof is filled with wire netting. The floors of the pens can be boarded or simply made of sand, but the hallway must have a board floor to facilitate cleaning and because the board floor affords better footing for the attendant.

Following is the bill of lumber and other material required for building this house, together with a statement of the use to which each lot of lumber, wire netting, etc., is put: 1530 feet of hemlock boards for sheathing and flooring; 525 feet of white pine for siding; 4 pieces of 4 x 4 x 16 for sills; 2 pieces of 4 x 4 x 14 for sills; 14 pieces 2 x 6, 14 feet long for floor joists; 16 pieces 2 x 4, 12 feet long for studding; 24 pieces 2 x 4, 10 feet long, for rafters; 9 pieces 2 x 4, 16 feet long for interior studding; 16 pieces 1 x 6, 8 feet long and 8 pieces 1 x 3, 8 feet long for nests and drop board supports; 24 pieces 15 inches long and 2 feet wide for nest divisions; 8 pieces 2 x 4, 1½ feet long to support nests and drop boards and nest bottoms; 8 pieces 2 x 2, 8 feet long, half round, for perches; 68 linear feet, 1 x 3, for doors;

COOPS AND EQUIPMENT.

24 square feet 2-inch wire mesh for doors; 24 feet 2-inch wire mesh for pen divisions; 22 feet 2-inch wire mesh for space above drop boards; 5 rolls 3-ply roofing; 4 pieces, 1 x 12, 8 feet long for partitions, 24 hinges, nails, screws, etc.

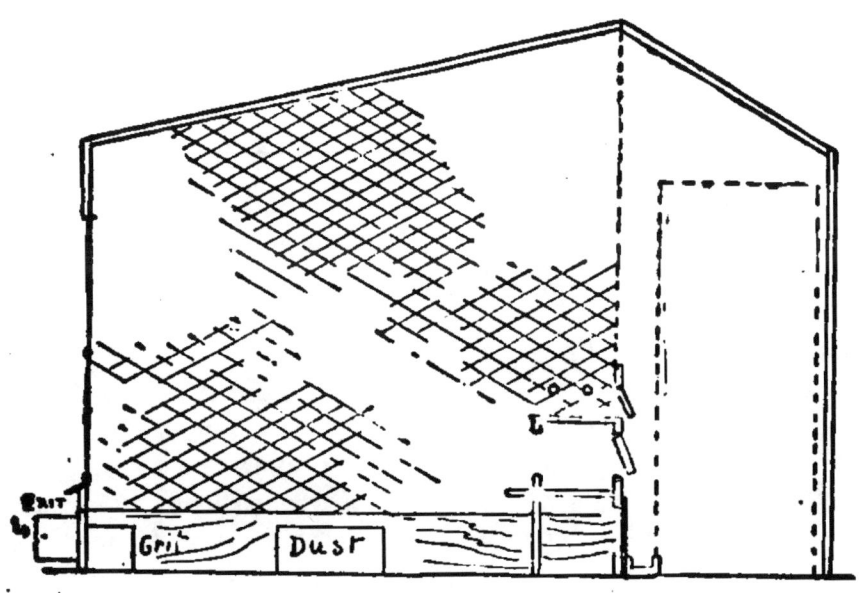

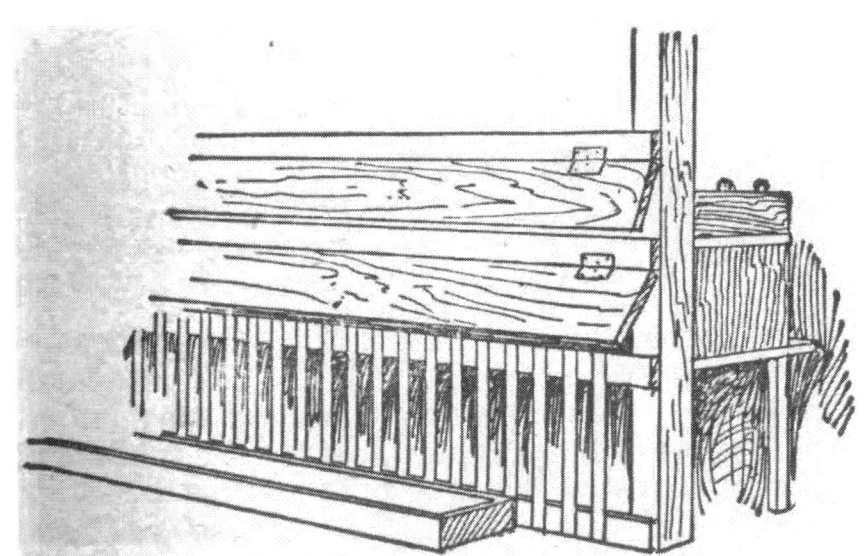

Cross Section and Drawing Showing Partition Between Pens and Hallway, Indicating the Location of Fixtures and Utensils in the House Designed by A. K. Johnson.

A SLANT FRONT HOUSE.

A Slanting Front and Consequently a Small Roof Area are Claimed to be Advantages.

By N. J. Holden, Minnesota.

For several years I have carefully studied to find how I could build a good, comfortable building for the least amount of money. I can build a building of this kind (see the accompanying illustrations) cheaper than I can build a continuous house with scratching sheds at the ends of the roosting pens. By having the front slanting I get a good sized floor space and at the same time a small roof which will save expense. I can also have the rear of the building low which again saves expense and makes the roosting room warmer. The passage way is wide enough so that a wheelbarrow can be used when cleaning out the building.

Exterior of "A Slant Front House" Designed by N. J. Holden.

The house can be built with single walls, except the north wall in the roosting room which should be double boarded with tar paper between. A curtain on a roll may be used to let down in front of the roosting table during cold nights.

I prefer the following way of building this house: A small foundation of stone or brick should be set in the ground 8 x 12 inches. I would have a floor in the roosting room, but not in the scratching room shed. I would sheet the building up on the outside with drop siding, on the inside of which I would place good tar felt. I would lath and plaster all the walls with hard plaster but would nail common boards under the roof, not placing them close together, and fill the space between them and the roof with

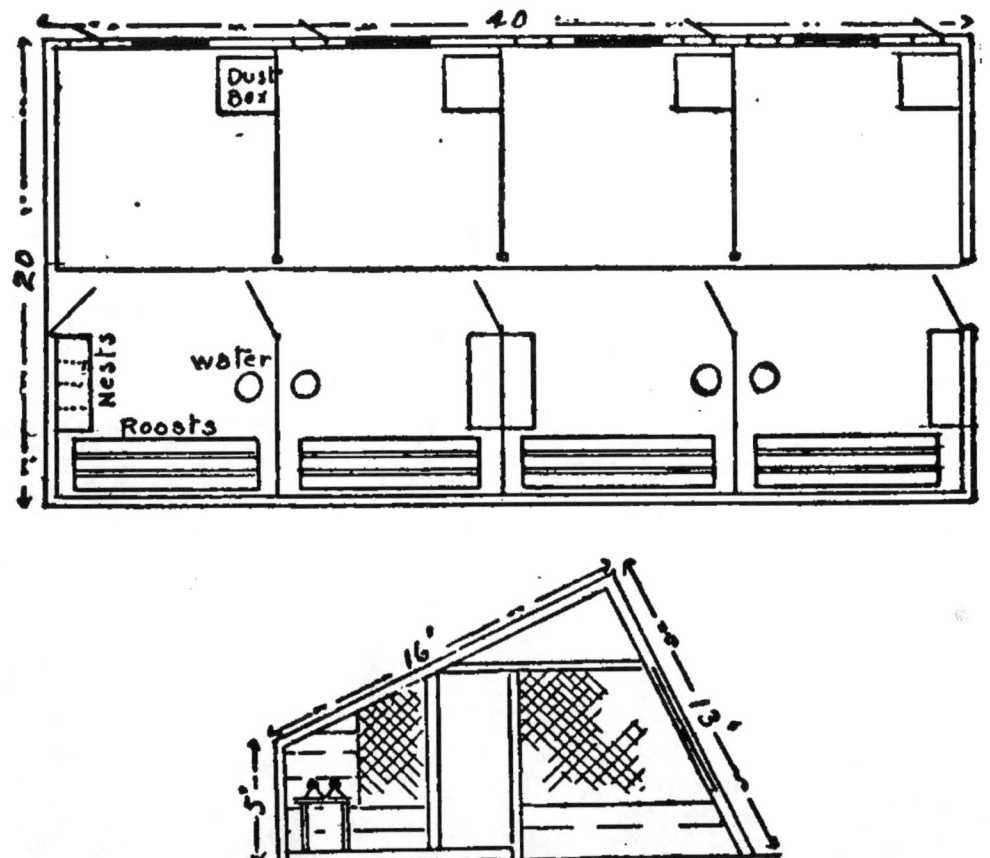

Ground Plan and Cross Section of "A Slant Front House" Designed by N. J. Holden.

straw, my experience having indicated that this is a perfect way to make the building free from dampness. You will notice the two small doors, hung at the top, on the end of the house. The opposite end is the same. The large door is to ventilate the building, and the smaller one to ventilate the space above the ceiling, if necessary. I would use common boards and good tar felt and cedar shingles for the roof.

Another way to build this house is to raise the passage

way 10 to 12 inches from the floor so the birds can pass under it in going between the roosting room and the scratching room. Wire partitions should separate this walk from the pens on each side, with doors to each pen. The passage way will then be separated and the work may be done more easily, but the cost of construction will be slightly higher. The nests might be so placed that the eggs could be gathered from the walk.

The front and rear sills are 4 x 4, but could be made of two pieces of 2 x 4, if more convenient. The two end sills are to be of 2 x 4, spiked to the ends of the 4 x 4 and to the ends of the 2 x 4 floor joists. On the top of all window casings should be nailed a piece of tin two or three inches wide to both sheeting and casing to prevent the rain from driving in on top of the window. A piece of tin should also be used in like manner at the bottom of each window.

View of "Continuous House for Winter Layers," Recommended by C. A. Pfeiffer.

CONTINUOUS HOUSE FOR WINTER LAYERS.

This House Will Comfortably Accommodate Thirty-Five Layers in Each Pen During the Winter Months.

By C. A. Pfeiffer, Minnesota.

The large continuous house illustrated herewith is my winter laying house. It is 16 x 12 feet. Each pen will accommodate thirty-five layers comfortably when confined during the winter months. The building rests on a stone foundation and is well constructed throughout. The sills are 4 x 6 inches, studding and rafters 2 x 4, placed 2 feet apart.

On the studding we first tack frost proof paper, ⅝ of an inch thick, then sheet with 6-inch drop siding and cover with two coats of paint. The inside walls are sheeted up with common boards surfaced, and the space between studs is packed with bale shavings. The ceiling and roof boards are of 6-inch flooring; the space between is packed with shavings. The roof is covered with 3-ply tar felt. There are two windows in each pen, the upper one being 2 x 4 feet in size and the lower 3 x 4 feet, both hung on hinges for convenience in ventilating, cleaning out litter, etc. Two roosts, made of 2 x 4 pieces, 12 feet long, are placed on the north side of each pen. Droppings boards are 8 inches below the roosts and the nest boxes are directly under the droppings boards. All the above fixtures are removable, making it an easy matter to keep down vermin. There are no floors used; just plain ground filled in level with the top of the stone walls. The entire floor space is used for scratching room.

This house is comfortably warm in the coldest weather and the hens never fail to give the most gratifying results in winter eggs. All the work was hired done at a time when labor was high and the building cost, approximately, $250.00 but our White Wyandottes paid for it in winter eggs in two seasons. We house our prospective layers early, generally in October, start them laying early, keep them at it all winter and when the price of eggs gets too low to suit us, sell off all surplus stock and use part of the house, with yards attached, for our breeding pens.

For use in warmer latitudes, this house could be built with one thickness of boards on the outside of the frame and be made wind and water proof by covering it with tar felt or with clapboards. Or, the house could be covered with drop siding and lined with the tar felt. This manner of building would reduce the cost of the house considerably.

By way of digression, we had 102 pullets and a few old hens (reserved for breeders) that shelled out 2,063 eggs during the month of January, 1906, which is a record anyone may be proud of.

We find that it pays to keep our layers in warm houses because less of the food is needed to produce heat and a greater proportion can go to produce eggs.

Illustration Showing Partition, Fixtures and Utensils in one Pen of "Continuous House for Winter Layers," Recommended by C. A. Pfeiffer.

HOUSE WITHOUT ROOST PLATFORMS.

The Designer Discards Droppings Boards, but Adopts Many Labor Saving Conveniences.

By F. Leggo, Minnesota.

The diagram shows a plan for a continuous poultry house for two pens of eighteen to twenty fowls each. It may be enlarged by adding any number of pens built alike.

The dimensions are 12 x 28 feet on the ground, outside measurement, 6 feet high on front or south side, 7 feet high on rear or north side, 9 feet high 3½ feet from rear wall, making a gable over the passage way. It has a stone foundation and dirt floor. The framework is of 2 x 4 stuff. The sides and partitions are of unmatched pine boards, dressed on one side, put on with boards running up and down and the cracks covered with battens. It is lined with tarred paper and roofed with shingles or roofing felt. The windows in front are 24 x 30 inches, 15 inches from the floor. It is ventilated by muslin frames in openings 2 x 3 feet between the windows in each pen, 3 feet from the floor, fitted with wooden doors which may be opened or closed according to the weather.

The entire floor space is available for scratching, making a scratching floor 8½ x 14 feet in each pen. The roosts are 18 inches from the floor and 18 inches above the roosts is a platform, 3 feet wide, on top of which are the nests. The hens get up to the platform by a runway or board with cleats nailed on it. Back of the nests is an opening covered with a long board on hinges, so the eggs can be gathered from the passage way. The front of the platform has a railing made of lath or wire netting, so the hens will have to go up and down by the runway and will not be likely to hurt themselves flying down to the floor, and will not be so likely to want to roost on the platform. In cold weather a curtain is let down from the front and end of the platform in front of and at the end of the roosts. In the end of each pen is a cage made of lath or netting, 2 feet wide, 8½ feet long and 2 feet from floor, for surplus males or for breaking up broody hens.

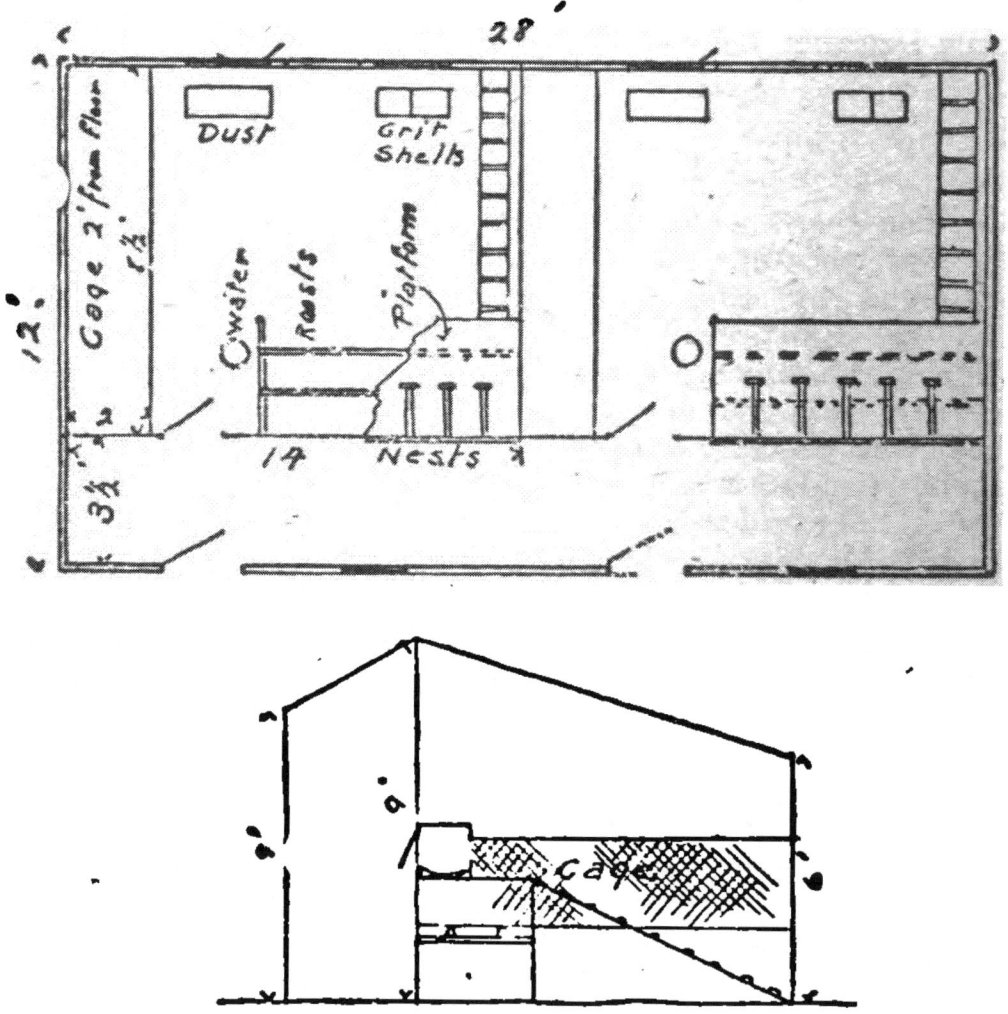

Floor Plan and Cross Section of F. Leggo's "House Without Roost Platforms."

No droopings boards are used, the droopings mixing with the litter which is raked from the under roosts every day and changed when necessary. In the passage way there is room for keeping feed, coops, etc., with windows in the wall for light. Dust box, grit and shell boxes and water fountain are placed as shown in diagram.

A WOMAN'S POULTRY HOUSE.

The Description of a Continuous Poultry House that Proves Satisfactory in South Dakota.

By Mrs. F. Studt, South Dakota.

Our poultry house is 16 x 48 feet and according to some writers should be divided in three pens for 150 chickens; we have it divided into four pens. We selected a well drained spot upon which to build and my husband, a farmer, built the foundation wall himself. He dug a trench and placed boards on each side, then filled it with rocks and filled the whole with sidewalk cement. After this hardened the boards were removed, leaving a good wall that rats cannot dig through. The wall is a foot high above the ground. The sills are made of 2 x 6 and 2 x 4 spiked together; the studding is 6 feet high, made of 2x6 joists, placed four feet apart. The building has a gable roof extending east and west, the windows facing the south. The studding was sheeted inside and out with rough lumber from an old barn and then packed tightly with flax straw and care taken to close it tightly at top so mice can not get in between the walls. It was then sheeted inside and out with roofing felt; the 3-ply felt was used outside and on the roof and the 2-ply was used inside. Shingles and board siding is preferred for the outside, but the felt was used to save cost. The felt is excellent inside to keep out vermin and cold and can be painted with tar paint or whitewashed. Over head are boards laid an inch or more apart and the space above is filled with straw. Sliding small doors are placed in the east and west ends of the gable for ventilators. We find this a very good plan to keep out frost in winter and heat in summer.

We have two entry doors, one east and one west, 3 feet wide. The pens are separated with poultry netting with a board at the bottom about a foot high. The first pen on the east is boarded up for a brood pen. Each pen has three windows, each with eight lights, 8 x 10 glass. They are all double; the inside are two-piece windows, and one outside window in each pen is hinged to open for ventilation. In the center, above each three windows, is a small burlap window for ventilation, made to close in the coldest weather. Below the windows in each pen are slides to open and close by weights on ropes and pulleys. All the doors are in the south ends of the partitions.

The north end is used for roosts. The droppings boards are made of shiplap put together with pitch to keep out

Exterior of "A Woman's Poultry House." Note the Ventilating Areas over the Windows and in the Gable.

vermin; they are 2 feet from the tops of the sills and 5 feet wide. These reach across the north sides of the pens. The roosts are a foot above the droppings boards; they consist of 2 x 2 pieces, the first one set 10 inches from the wall and the others 12 inches apart. The arms on which the roosts rest are hinged to the wall so the whole may be raised to clean the droppings boards. These are of 2 x 4 with places sawed out to fit the 2 x 2 roosts, which can be lifted out for special cleaning. I think a better way is to have the roosts run the short way of the platform so the chickens cannot crowd so much; it is some more work but well worth it. Burlap curtains should be used in front of the roosts at night in real cold weather. Underneath the front of the droppings boards we have a long bench with a platform facing north. This bench is divided with boards into ten nests and the droppings boards serve for the top. A long board hinged to the bench on the south side serves for the back of the nests when closed and fastened against a 2 x 4 underneath the front of droppings board. This board can be let down to gather the eggs and the bench can be carried out for special cleaning.

We have a hard packed ground floor and keep it covered with clean straw or millet hay when we have it. They do not scratch this up like a sand floor. We thought of cement-

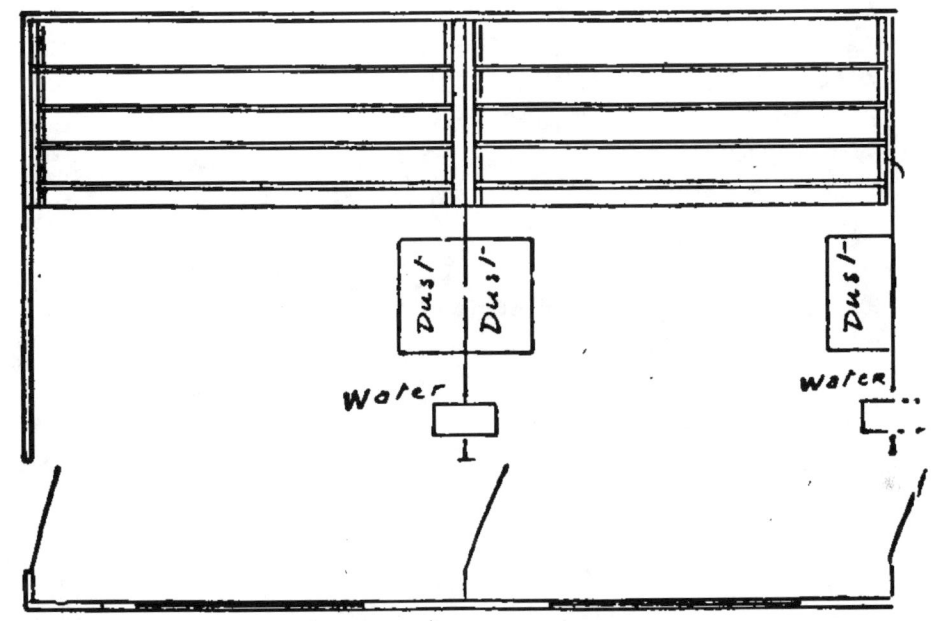

Illustration Showing the Location of Roosts, Roost Platforms, Dust Baths, Water Pans, etc., in "A Woman's Poultry House."

ing all but four feet on the south side which we were going to leave for dust boxes but, the ground floor works so well we have given up the idea of cementing it. We made good sized frames to place on the ground for dust boxes in which we sift all our ashes and have some earth mixed with it, and occasionally some lime. We keep the dust boxes cleaned of the droppings with the sifter. The chickens seem to take much pleasure in these boxes. I often see half a dozen in at a time and let me say here, get a barrel of good lime and put it in the hen house and use it as slacks. Sifted over the droppings boards after they are cleaned, also the roosts and nest boxes, it is the cheapest and best thing known to rid the house and keep it rid of vermin. We have a neighbor whose fowls were bothered by red mites and who used whitewash, kerosene etc., but said it seemed he could not get rid of them. He was told to use lime in the above way and says he is not bothered with mites now. I keep watching for vermin on my fowls but fail to find any and believe the use of these dust boxes, cared for as they should be, is the easiest way to keep fowls rid of pests. We have galvanized drinking founts made to order, one for two pens placed in a box in an opening in the partition so a part of it is on each side. We have feeders, home made, to hang on the wall for grit, oyster shell and feed.

Our hen house cost $150.00, but would have cost more if we had not had some old barn lumber to use. My husband did not have time to build the house himself and the labor hired amounted to $75.00.

If this house were simply single boarded, on the outside of the frame, and covered with 3-ply felt the cost of building it would be a good many dollars less. A house so constructed would do very well in warm climates but we prefer the double wall for use in South Dakota where the temperature gets pretty low and where the winds are strong.

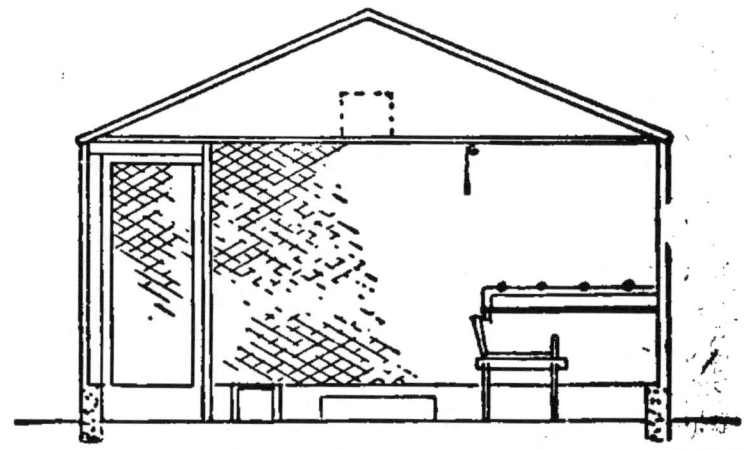

Drawing of Cross Section of "A Woman's Poultry House," Showing Partition, Location of Roosts, Nests, etc.

A FANCIER'S POULTRY HOUSE.

An Inexpensive, Convenient, Healthful Building that Provides Accommodations for Breeding Pens and Fowls Intended for Exhibition.

By F. H. Williams, Minnesota.

This plan embraces, in my opinion, all that is necessary for the welfare of the fowls it is intended to house and at the same time is convenient for the attendant.

The total length of the house is 52 feet. It faces the south and is what I term a combination of glass and muslin front. Thirty-two feet of the length is built 8 feet wide, 7 feet high in front, 5 feet at the rear and is divided into three pens, one 12 feet, the other two 10 feet long. At the east end the building is enlarged to 14 x 16 feet and is 8 feet high to the plates, with a peak roof. This part of the building is designed for the use of the show birds. The entire rear wall above the roosts is covered with single coops, size 2 x 2½ feet each. The sides of this room are arranged in the same way. Roosts and droppings boards are built at the extreme back of each pen with nests underneath the droppings boards, so built that they are above the floor and hens enter from the rear. A 12-inch board the width of the pen in length and hinged to the front edge of the droppings board covers the nests in front. This board is raised when collecting eggs. A curtain can be hung in front of roosts, but in using this type of house this last winter I did not once find use for the curtain during the entire winter.

Water can, feed, grit, oyster shells, scrap and charcoal boxes are hung around the sides of each pen, and the dust box is also built above the floor against one side of each pen. This leaves the entire floor space clear for scratching. Doors 3 feet wide and in a direct line with each other lead from one pen to another. Partitions between pens are solid, hence, there can be no draughts. A glance at the plan will show the arrangement of the front of the house. The windows are 3 x 4 and the doors 3 x 6, doors being made of frames covered with wire netting and muslin. Windows are hinged and swung upward and in. The doors will admit just the right amount of fresh air day and night and with

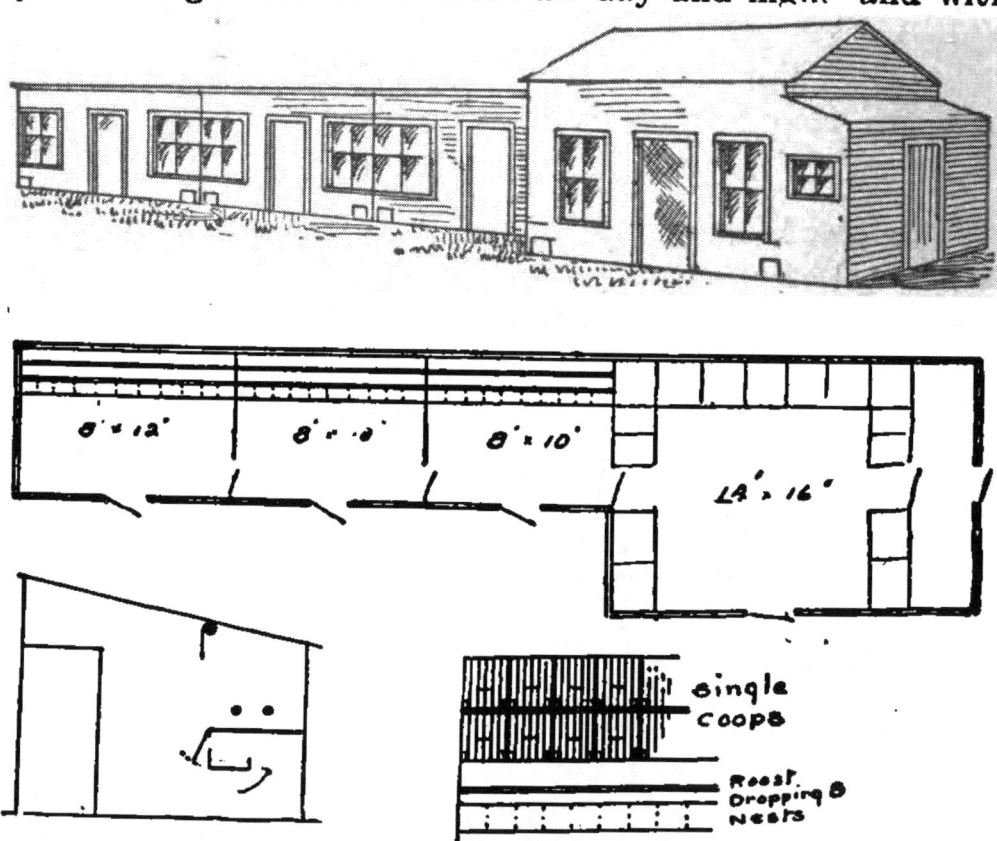

Perspective and Illustrations Showing the Manner of Constructing "A Fancier's Poultry House." Designed, Built and Used by F. H. Williams. Note the Arrangement of Fixtures.

the sunlight streaming through the windows during the day, it makes a combination that will cause the "biddies" to sing all day and that will bring the eggs also. The house is covered with a prepared roofing material all over, roof, sides and ends, and is water proof and wind proof. The floors are of wood, raised about one foot off the ground. The house is built almost entirely of old lumber and is inexpensive especially if one does the work himself.

In deciding on this type of house, I did so only after

giving two different styles a test this last winter. I find that the combination house, combining glass windows with the muslin front is far superior to an all muslin front or an all window front. There will be no frost on the walls with this style and no moisture, as the muslin doors will fill the house with pure, fresh air and the glass in the windows warm it to just the right degree of temperature to keep the fowls in perfect health. In the show bird room at the end of the building we have a room that is a necessity to one who is raising fancy stock for exhibition. Here the birds are trained in single coops, the same size they will be in at the shows. This room is also used for an ordinary pen as the coops for show stock are all arranged above the roosts and around the sides of the room. The drawing herewith will give one an idea of the arrangement. In this room the walls are 8 feet high to the plates and the upper part, or loft, is filled with loose straw, making it just as warm as the balance of the house that has the low roof.

All told, this house is all one could ask for, being low in cost, easy to build, warm enough for the fowls, has plenty of light and air and is very convenient for the attendant. I used one the past winter, a 24-foot house of practically the same type, except it had a cement floor, and did not have a sick bird or a frozen or frosted comb during the entire winter, and got a good supply of eggs at the same time.

COOPS AND EQUIPMENT

COOP WITH PLATFORM ROOST.

A Roosting Coop with a Raised Platform in the Center to Prevent Crowding in the Corners.

By Louis Riedesel, North Dakota.

This roosting coop is 4 x 8 feet on the ground and the sides are 2 feet high. The roof has a one-third pitch and is shingled. The sides are covered with shiplap and siding. There is one small window in each end and a hole for ventilation above each window. There is also a small opening in one side through which the chicks pass in going in and out of the coop.

The floor, as shown on the illustration, is made separate from the rest of the coop and is raised 3 inches from the ground leaving a space 8 inches wide on each side and each end. The building can be lifted from this platform, or floor, and the latter may be easily cleaned. This makes a warm, dry place, perfectly safe for chicks, which will not pile up in one corner as they all get on the raised platform.

It will accommodate about seventy-five chicks from the time they leave the brooder until they are old enough to go to roost in the larger houses.

(It will be noted that the raised platform takes the place of roosts in this plan. If to be used in midsummer the coop would require better facilities for ventilating or the chicks would overheat and perhaps some would suffo-

COOPS AND EQUIPMENT. 71

cate. One of the greatest barriers to successful chicken raising is a summer coop without all, or nearly all, of the front side open.—Editor.)

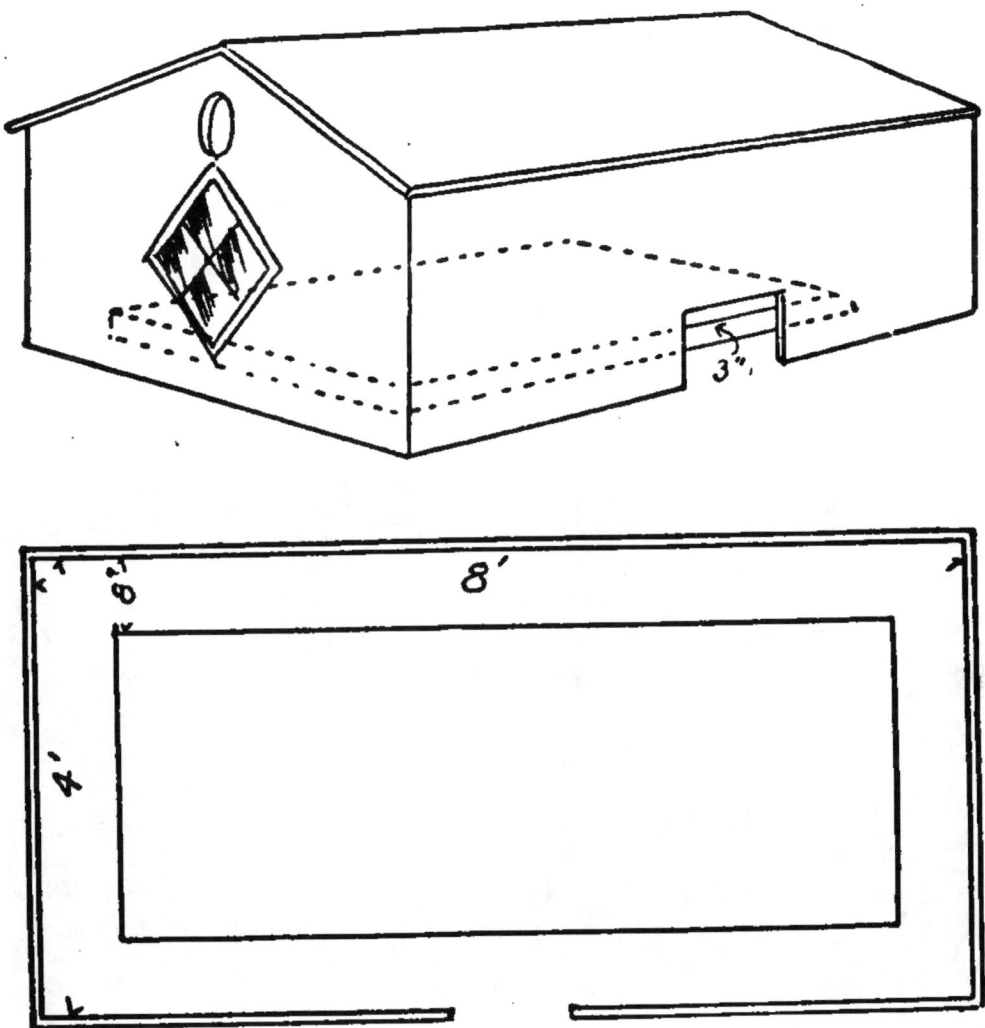

Illustration Showing the Construction of "Coop With Platform Roost," Designed by Louis Riedesel, to Prevent Chickens Crowding in the Corners.

AN OPEN FRONT ROOSTING COOP.

A Well Ventilated Coop to Accommodate Fifty Chickens During the Summer and Fall.

By H. A. Nourse, Minnesota.

This substantial, practical coop is 6 feet long, 4 feet wide, 4 feet high in front and 2½ feet high at the back. The sills are of 2 x 4 stuff and the plates of 2 x 3. There are no posts or studs; the boarding, which is of ⅞ tongued and grooved lumber, makes the coop sufficiently strong without them. The sides are boarded up and down and the

A Well Ventilated Roosting Coop, Described by H. A. Nourse.

roof and floor are boarded crosswise. The roof is made water proof by covering with tar paper or one of the prepared roofings made and advertised for use on poultry houses. The front is entirely of slats, placed up and down, 2 inches apart.

To keep out hostile animals, including skunks, rats, weasels, etc., inch mesh wire is fastened in front of the slats with cleats as shown on the accompanying illustration.

While the chicks are young no roosts are placed in this coop, but in the fall when the chicks are sufficiently developed so that roosting will not injure them, 2 x 3 pieces with corners rounded and of the length that will set between the ends of the coop are placed in each coop. These are supported by cleats nailed inside the ends. This structure will accommodate fifty chicks from the time they are weaned by the hen or removed from the brooder until they are placed in permanent houses in the fall.

To prevent storms from driving in and to keep out the cold, which sometimes overtakes the poultryman before his fall work is done and the chicks moved to winter quarters, a burlap curtain may be placed over the front of this coop at night.

A SANITARY BROOD COOP.

Directions and Bill of Material Required for Constructing a Coop Costing $2.23.

By P. F. Tassie, Minnesota.

The photos herewith presented show a brood coop for either a hen and chicks or for chicks alone after leaving the brooder. This was especially designed by the writer as a sanitary brood coop.

The construction is as follows: 6-inch flooring is used throughout and the coop is 3 feet long, 2½ feet wide, 2½ feet high in front and 2 feet high in the rear, which gives the roof a 6-inch pitch. The floor space is about 8 square feet.

To make the coop, take three pieces of 2 x 4 and place them with the narrow edges up, one piece along the back and one piece on each side, leaving the front open to admit air and keep the floor dry. To this 2 x 4 framework is nailed the flooring and upon this a frame work of 2 x 2 is made and the walls are then nailed on. In the front wall, a foot from either side, a door is cut the height of the first two boards, 12 inches. This door is a foot wide and is hinged on the floor; it opens outward and forms the running board to the ground.

We do not board the front clear to the top, but leave an open space 6 inches wide and extending clear across the top of the coop. This is covered with wire screening to keep out cats and other animals and affords ample ventilation. This aids in the growth of the chicks.

At the rear the first two boards are nailed together and then hinged to the floor. This is the "clean-out" door and opens down to the ground. This enables one to get into each corner and clean it thoroughly and is one of the the best features of the coop.

The roof is made to extend about 6 inches over the rear of the coop and 2 to 3 inches on each side. A board is then placed at an angle over the front where we have the wire covered space, so that no water will get in, and the roof is covered with tar paper or shingles.

The coop is then painted any color to suit one's taste. Mine are painted buff and present a very neat and attractive appearance on the green lawn or in the orchard. If painted

Photograph Showing Manner of Cleaning the Floor of "A Sanitary Brood Coop."

COOPS AND EQUIPMENT. 75

"A Sanitary Brood Coop" with Removable Yard in Front.

every two years they will last an indefinite length of time.

A run is made the width of the coop and about 6 to 8 feet long by nailing pieces of 2 x 4 together, erecting a frame of 2 x 2 stuff on this and covering with wire netting, inch mesh on the sides and the ordinary poultry netting on top.

A frame door, or lid, is made 18 inches wide and extending across the end of the run nearest the coop. This is made of 2 x 2 stuff and covered with wire and enables you to place water and feed in the run and also enables you to open and close the door in the front of the coop.

The material required and cost of same for making the coop and run is as follows: 35 square feet 6-inch flooring, 80 cents; 45 linear feet 2 x 4 and 35 linear feet 2 x 2, 60 cents; 8 square feet tar paper, 5 cents; wire for run, 50 cents; 2 pairs hinges, 8 cents; nails, etc., 10 cents; paint, 10 cents. Total, $2.23.

MOVABLE ROOSTING COOP.

A Practical Commodious Coop Designed to be Hauled from Place to Place by a Horse.

By C. E. Barnes, Washington.

This roosting coop is 5 x 8 feet on the ground, 5 feet high in front and 3½ feet high behind. It is built of dressed and matched lumber and the roof is made water proof by covering with a prepared roofing. It will accommodate from one hundred to one hundred fifty chickens. It is built on 2 x 4 sills, the side sills extending one foot beyond the building at one end. These are rounded up at the points like sled runners and a cross bar is nailed on so that the coop may be hauled from place to place by a horse. There is a window in the front side to furnish light and opening for the chicks to pass in and out on each side

The roosts extend the full length of the coop and when the chicks are first put in they are placed only 1½ inches apart so that the chicks cannot fall through while learning to roost. Later they are moved so that they will be 3 inches apart and later still they are separated by 6 inch spaces and are left in that position until the chicks are old enough to go into the regular hen house.

This coop has no floor and the droppings fall on the ground, so all that is required to clean the coop is to move it to a fresh location.

(We believe that the designer of this coop does not intend to advise anyone to keep as many as one hundred or more chicks in it until they are old enough to be removed, or until the advance of winter compels the owner to remove them. It appears to us that fifty chicks would be as many as could be comfortably housed in a coop of these dimensions. We suggest also that in most parts of this country a larger window or more open space in front should be provided for better ventilation during the hot nights that most chicks have to go through.—Editor.)

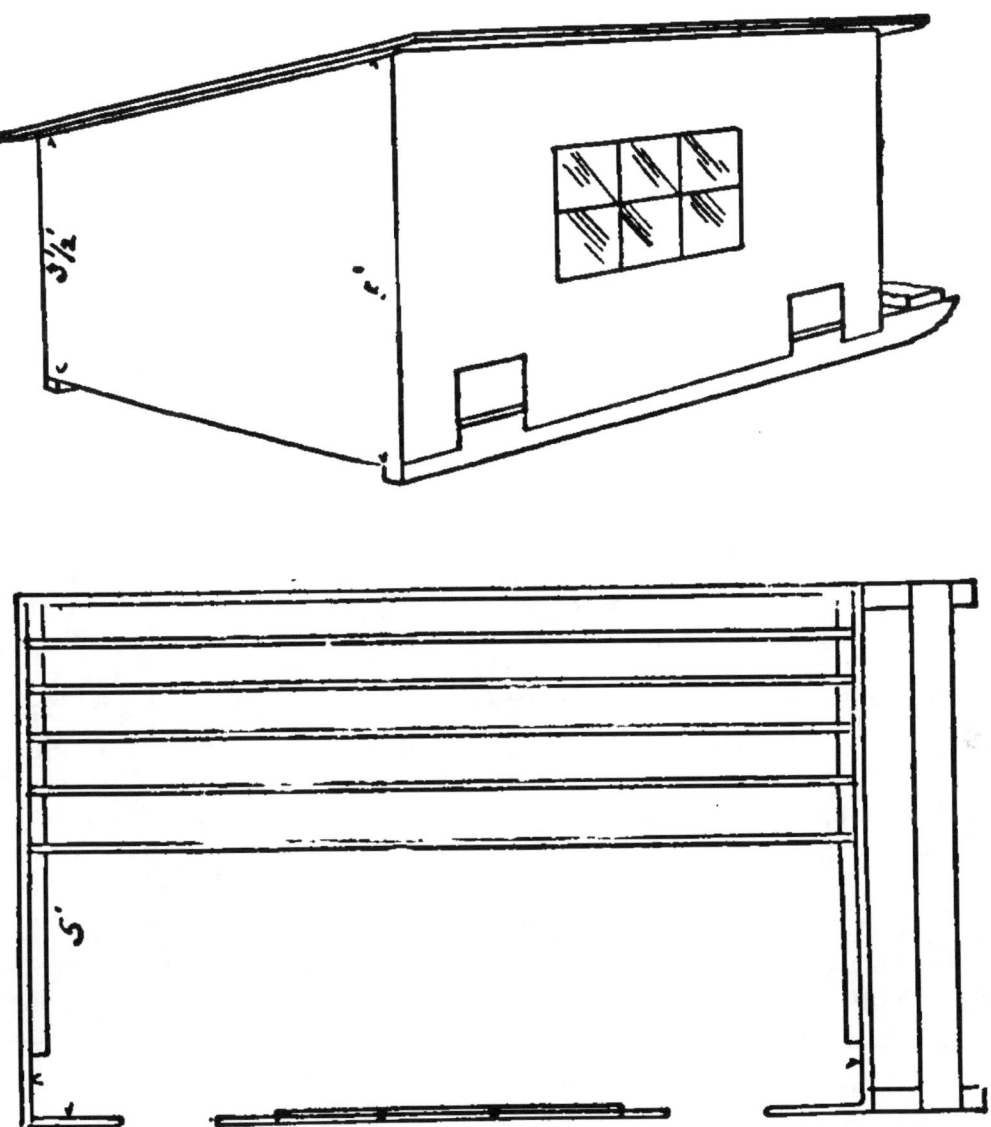

Roosting Coop Designed by C. E. Barnes. The Upper Illustration Shows the Coop Complete with Runners upon which it is Hauled About; the Lower Shows the Roosts and their Supports.

A COLD WEATHER ROOSTING COOP.

Description of a Roosting Coop that is Capable of Being Well Ventilated or Closed Quite Tightly, According to the Weather.

By H. A. Nourse, Minnesota.

It frequently happens that the number of fowls on hand, or the press of other work, prevents the poultryman from getting his chicks into winter quarters in permanent houses before the weather becomes quite cold in the fall. Then about the first of October, too, the nights begin to get cold and the open front roosting coop does not afford sufficient protection against cold rains or winds. These coops should be provided with a burlap or muslin curtain which can be let down in front when conditions require it, but even then, they do not afford comfortable quarters in the cold weather that follows. Sometimes there is an advantage in keeping the growing chicks in roosting coops until the arrival of actual winter weather. This is particularly true when by placing them in permanent houses we curtail their range to yards that are of small area or bare of grass, or both.

Free range in the fields is beneficial so long as the chicks have comfortable roosting places at night and the temperature is not uncomfortably cool in the day time. These conditions are easily secured when one has mowing lands or pastures or even a couple of city lots and a roosting coop so built that it can be closed fairly tight at night when the weather is cold or opened to admit plenty of fresh air when the weather is warm. Such a coop should be 6 feet long and 4 feet wide for twenty-five chicks, and may be made of tongued and grooved lumber and have its roof covered with tar paper or some other weather proof fabric to make it tight.

An excellent coop for this purpose is illustrated here.

COOPS AND EQUIPMENT.

This coop is 4 x 6 feet on the ground, 4 feet high in front, and 3 feet high at the back. Very little frame is required in this structure, simply the sills at the bottom and plates at the top to nail the sides and ends to. The floor is nailed on the sills and the roof to the plates. No posts are required at the corners, but the boards are nailed firmly together which gives the coop sufficient strength. There is a door 18 inches wide in the front, near one end, and a window 3 feet long and 15 inches high, also in the front, near the top. This window is covered on the outside with wire netnetting to keep the chicks in and hostile animals out. Inside of

"A Cold Weather Roosting Coop," described by H. A. Nourse.

this netting, a frame filled with cotton cloth is hung on hinges at its base so that it may be swung entirely open or only part way, according to the requirements. When this clothfilled frame is entirely closed, all drafts are shut out, but plenty of air is admitted for the chicks to breathe. This should not, however, be entirely closed except in below-freezing weather. Beneath the window, near the floor, is a small door for the chickens, which can be closed at night. This coop may be placed on runners if desired, so that it may be hauled from place to place by a horse.

The cost of constructing this coop is usually about $6.00 if the owner does the work himself and makes no charge for his labor. If painted, it will last many years. The sills should not be allowed to rest on the ground but should be placed on flat stones so that they will not decay from coming in eontact with the sod. The writer at one time, used fifty of these roosting coops and placed them about the farm, about one hundred yards apart. The chicks were placed in them from the more open front coops, about the middle of September or the first of October and kept in them until very near the first of December, depending upon the severity of the weather. Occasionally these coops were used for quarters for cockerels until after Christmas. They were usually drawn to a point near the main buildings of the plant and placed in a row, end to end. The north sides and the ends were banked with straw or swale hay to protect them from the north and west winds. The floors were covered with 2 inches of sand which was in turn, covered with straw or hay to a depth of 3 or 4 inches to serve as scratching material. From five to eight cockerels were kept in each coop and the results, at least so far as influence of the coops was concerned, were satisfastory.

There is little comparison between the growth and development of the chick on free range in the late fall and that of the one confined in small yards. The former will not only grow faster, but will develop more uniformly and build up a more robust constitution. Moreover, there is a considerable saving of food. Dried berries, seeds, bugs and worms, grass, etc., are consumed by the free range chick in considerable quantities and take the place of much of the purchased grain that would be required to feed a flock confined in yards.

Occasionally, in the late fall, there will be a day when a cold rain or perhaps a light fall of snow, will make it necessary for these youngsters to be confined to the coop. On such days, hay, straw or leaves should be placed several inches deep on the floor to provide a place in which to bury

COOPS AND EQUIPMENT.

grain in order that the chicks may be kept busy scratching for it. When these free range chicks are fed with automatic feeders it is necessary to visit the coops but twice a day; once in the morning to let out the chicks and give them water, as well as to clean the coop, and once at night to close the coop and adjust doors and windows for ventilation. Where it is not necessary to shut the chicks in the coop at night once a day is sufficient to visit the coops, at which time they can be cleaned, fresh water furnished and the feeders filled, if necessary.

We once saw some of these coops used for winter quarters for a pen of laying hens and later the same season for a breeding pen. Two of them were placed end to end and were covered with tar paper well cleated. A hole was cut from one into the other and one was used as a roosting and laying pen, the other for a scratching shed. Eight hens and a male were kept in each house thus made. Cloth windows were used and in the scratching pen, a cloth filled frame took the place of the door.

It appears from the foregoing, that it is possible to make good use of these coops in every season and that pullets may be placed in them in the fall and carried right through to the next fall, with comfort to them and satisfaction to the owner.

A DRY GOODS BOX COOP.

A Plan for Converting a Dry Goods Box into a Convenient and Healthful Coop for Growing Chicks.

By H. A. Nourse, Minnesota.

One of the best and cheapest roosting coops we have seen was made by the writer from a dry goods box which he purchased at a store for 20 cents, with the addition of a few pieces of waste lumber which he found about the place. To make this coop, place the box upon the widest side and remove the top and the front side down to within 4 or 6 inches of the ground. Saw a 6 inch board which is as long as the coop is wide from corner to corner and toenail each

Photograph of a Roosting Coop Made from a Dry Goods Box by H. A. Nourse.

piece to an end of the box, forming the slant for the roof. To support these boards in front, nail a wide piece on the front of the coop extending from the top of these pieces to a point 4 or 6 inches down the side of the box. Then take the boards removed from the front and top of the box and use them to make the roof, boarding up and down the slant.

The roof is covered with tar paper, firmly cleated and bent over the edge of the roof at the front, back and ends and secured by cleats to prevent any rain driving under it. The roosts rest on cleats nailed to the inside of each end and the door is made of slats or lath and arranged as shown in the illustration, so that it can be opened or shut by sliding it to one side.

When there is no danger that skunks or other animals will attack the chicks during the night, the floor may be removed from this coop which may be removed to a fresh location every morning, thus keeping it clean with the least labor.

BROOD COOP WITH SLIDING DOOR.

Directions for Building a Ventilated, Shed Roof Coop for Hen and Brood of Chicks.

By J. W. Bisping, Minnesota.

I will describe a coop for a hen and her brood which I bulit myself and find very satisfactory. The dimensions are: Length 4 feet, width 2 feet, height of front 2 feet, height of back 1 foot. It has a shed roof 5 x 3 feet, which allows for a considerable projection on all sides. In front is a door 1 foot high and the length of the coop which slides between cleats nailed to the outside and inside of the coop; this can be opened much or little as is desired. We open it a little at first so that the chicks can get out, but the hen is confined. When the young ones are ten days to two weeks old we let the hen out with them to scratch in the ground and enjoy the sunshine. In the front side, over the door, is an open space a foot long and 4 inches wide, covered

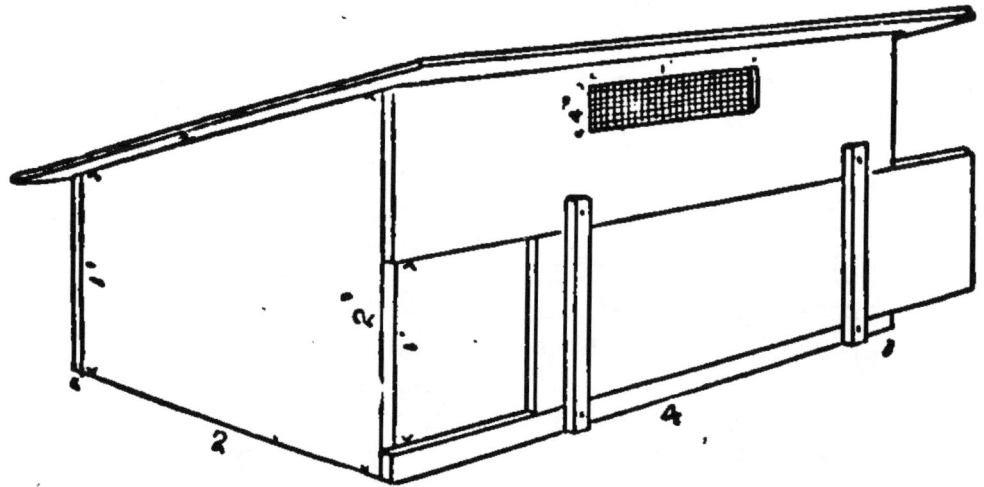

Drawing of "A Brood Coop with Sliding Door" Used and Recommended by J. W. Bisping.

with wire netting through which the air can pass in and out for ventilation.

I bed the floors with wheat chaff and place the coops on the sunny side of the poultry house. I set them on blocks about 4 inches from the ground, placing a slanting board in front for the chicks to run up and down. I built three of these coops last year and they are so satisfactory that I am building more this year.

HANDY BROOD COOP.

A Plan for Building a Brood Coop with Gable Roof and Removable Floor.

By Ross Haibeck, Minnesota.

To build this coop use tongued and grooved lumber ⅞ of an inch thick, dressed on both sides. Two boards 6 or 8 inches wide are sawed to make the gables on each end and the roof is nailed directly to these boards and then to the horizontal boards of the sides of the coop. Cleats of ⅞-inch board should be placed one in each corner and one across the lower edge of the front, inside, to support the front side between the doors. Cleats should also be placed vertically, one on the inner side of each door, inside the coop. There are two doors, one of which is hinged at the top and swings up to allow the chickens to run in and out between the slats that are behind it. The other is hinged at the side and is opened to allow the hen to go in and out or to allow the caretaker to reach in for any purpose

The floor is built on cleats and sits inside the house without being fastened to it; the object being to permit the removal of the house when it is desired to clean the floor. There is a small window in the front side to admit light. If this coop in used in summer when the nights are hot it is necessary to have it built more open in order to admit more air and so that it will not confine the heat. In several instances I have placed a hen and twenty to twenty-five chicks in a coop like this and have raised every one of the youngsters.

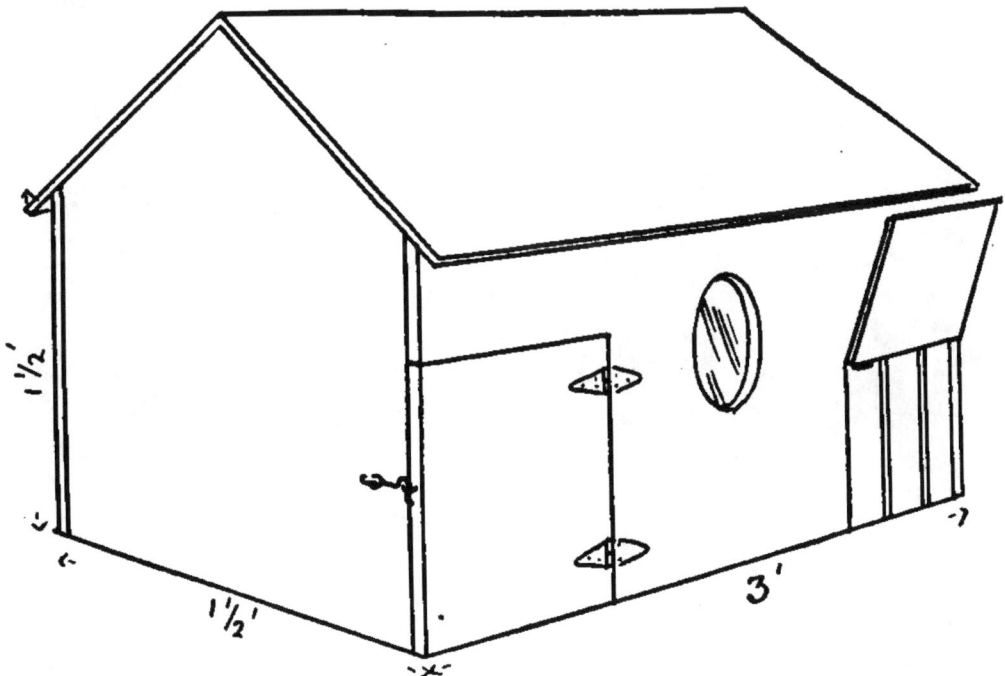

A Drawing of Ross Haibeck's "Handy Brood Coop."

BROOD COOP AND YARD.

How to Make a Simple and Inexpensive, Yet Satisfactory Coop and Yard for Hen and Chicks.

By H. A. Nourse, Minnesota.

Almost every poultry keeper has short pieces of board, left from the lumber used in the construction of larger buildings, which can be used to make coops for the hens with broods.

The accompanying illustration shows a coop two feet

An Inexpensive Brood Coop and Yard, Made Chiefly of Odds and Ends of Lumber, Designed by H. A. Nourse.

square, two feet high in front and eighteen inches at the rear. Narrow strips of inch board serve as posts at the corners and the boards are nailed firmly to them and to each other. The roof boards are nailed to the tops of the sides and ends and the roof is covered with water proof roofing fabric held in place by cleats.

The front is boarded down ten inches from the top and

the space below is occupied by laths placed upright, three inches apart. These laths are nailed to the inside of the front board at the top and to a narrow horizontal strip at the bottom, except one, which is held in place by cleats at top and bottom so that it can be easily removed when it is necessary to put in or take out the hen. The piece shown standing upright in front of the coop in the photo is not a part of it.

If a floor is used it may be made to fit inside the coop and be held together by cleats, so that the coop may be lifted off and the floor cleaned with convenience. Unless it is necessary to protect the brood from animals the floor may be dispensed with and the coop moved to a fresh place every day in lieu of cleaning it.

The yard is six feet long and four wide. The frame is made by nailing narrow pieces of inch board to corner posts of small dimension stuff, each post 14 inches long. Inch mesh wire netting, one foot wide, covers the sides and the same material with two-inch mesh covers the top. An open space is left near one corner where the yard sets against the coop.

BROOD COOP AND YARD.

A Plan for Making a Practical, Substantial Coop and Yard for a Hen and Brood of Chicks.

By H. P. Larson, South Dakota.

The accompanying illustration presents a brood coop that I am using on my farm. It is 32 inches wide and 34 inches long, 36 inches high in front and 22 inches at the rear. The sills are made of 2 x 2-inch stuff and the sides are of $7/8$ inch ceiling. The roof is of tongued and grooved roofing with battens on top. The sides are covered with water proof paper and the entire coop is painted on the outside with red roof paint. The floor is of flooring 8 inches wide and rests on the sills, making a 2-inch air space between the floor and the ground. The window in the front is a cellar sash containing three lights of 10 x 12 double glass. Above the window is an opening 12 inches wide, the full length of the coop, covered by a board hinged at the top. Back of this is a frame of inch mesh wire netting to keep out animals at night when the board is swung out for ventilation. Coops built like this can be used in the middle of the winter or in the hottest time in the summer as they can be closed up tight or opened to permit abundant air as the season requires.

For a yard I use, for the first few days, a strip of inch mesh wire netting 12 inches high, fastened to the coop at the ends and supported elsewhere by stakes driven in the ground. The coop and yard can be moved easily by one person when it is desired to change it to a fresh location. It is convenient in every way and very cheap; any sort of lumber can be used.

A better coop, one more healthful for the chicks and more convenient to use, would be difficult to find. The sliding window front makes it very easy to clean the floor by simply drawing out the accumulations with a hoe. The provision for ventilation is excellent and when the window is also opened it is practically an open front coop.—Editor.)

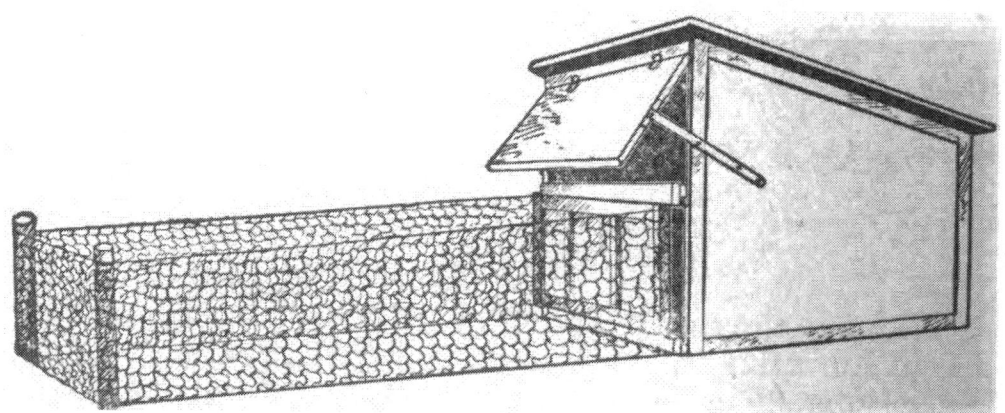

"Brood Coop and Yard" for Hen and Chicks. Designed by H. P. Larson.

POULTRY PLANT EQUIPMENT

Plans for Building Show Coops, Shipping Coops, Feed Troughs, Water Fountains, Roosts and Roost Platforms, Roost Curtains, Shelter Tents, Nests, Etc.

By H. A. Nourse.

The fixtures and utensils which we shall describe and illustrate are very simple and can be made by anyone who has the simplest carpenter's tools, including a hammer and saw. Some of them, show coops, shipping coops and water fountains for example, can sometimes be bought of poultry supply dealers cheaper than they can be made and regarding them we advise the poultryman to consult the dealers.

Exhibition Coops.

The principal requirements for a satisfactory exhibition coop are, that it be 2 feet long, 2 feet wide and 30 inches high for a single fowl (longer for pairs and pens) and that its front be so arranged that the birds can be viewed satisfactorily and with provision for easily removing the specimens for examination. A good coop built of light lumber is illustrated here (Fig. 1). It has a large vertical sliding door in front for introducing and removing the fowls and a horizontal door at the bottom, hinged at its top and fastened with a button at the bottom through which the floor may be easily cleaned. The same style of coop may be made by using light lumber to build a frame and covering

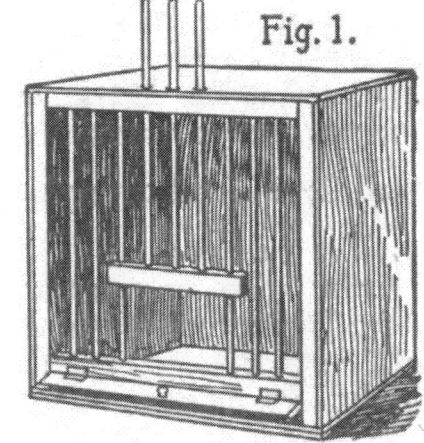
Fig. 1.

the frame, except the floor and front, with cotton cloth.

A Satisfactory Shipping Coop.

A shipping coop should have sufficient strength to make it a perfect protection for the fowls and at the same time be light enough to avoid excessive express charges. For shipping in the winter time, coops with solid wooden sides are preferred because they better protect the fowls against the cold winds on depot platforms and against the heat of steam pipes in express cars.

A coop for a single bird should be 12 inches wide, 18 inches long and 20 inches high. For large males with single combs, it is advisable to build coops 22 or 24 inches high to avoid the possibility of the specimen injuring his comb against the top. The coop we illustrate (Fig 2) has ends of ⅝ stuff and sides of ⅜ material. It is built wholly solid except the top which is covered with three slats, placed equally distant apart. No draft can reach a bird in such a coop though plenty of air will be admitted at the top. For summer use the sides of this coop should be made of ⅜ inch slats, 3 inches wide, placed half an inch apart. This mode of construction furnishes excellent ventilation, but does not allow the bird to put its head outside the coop where it might be injured during transportation.

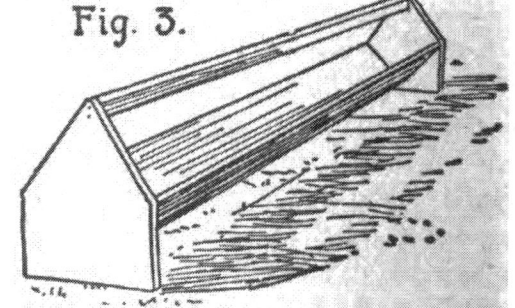

A Good Feed Trough.

The accompanying drawing (Fig. 3) illustrates a feed trough that is cheap and easy to construct and which the fowls can eat from easily, but cannot easily soil the food by getting into it. The trough is six inches wide and four inches deep and the ends project six inches above it, terminating in an angle. Between these angles is a piece of ⅞-inch board, 2 inches

COOPS AND EQUIPMENT.

wide, nailed through the ends in the same manner that the sides of the trough are fastened. The upper part of this 2-inch board is made with a sharp edge so that the fowls cannot stand upon it.

Some Home Made Water Fountains.

A very satisfactory watering device for little chicks is made by selecting two tin fruit cans, one having an inch greater diameter than the other. From the larger one, cut off one end, making a saucer an inch deep; cut off one end of the other at the joint of the side with the top or bottom, as the case may be, and cut one or two notches ¾ of an inch deep and perhaps an inch wide, as illustrated in Fig. 4. Now fill this can with water and place the saucer made from the larger can over it. Hold them tightly together, invert them and place on a level spot or on a piece of board. The water will flow into the saucer until the notches in the can are covered and will remain at that height in the saucer so long as the water remains in the can. It is necessary, of course, that the can be air tight for a leak will let in air and the water will overflow the saucer.

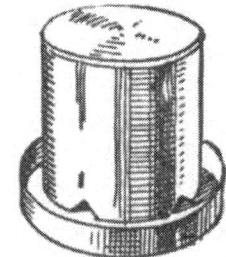

Fig. 4.

For use in poultry houses an open galvanized iron pan, like that illustrated in Fig. 5, is recommended. This pan can be made by any tinsmith and should correspond in size to the number of fowls in the flock to be watered. For ten fowls it should be made about 10 inches long at the bottom and 10½ inches at the top of the front side by 3½ inches wide at the bottom and 4 inches wide at the top. The back side should extend 1½ inches higher than the front and should have two holes, one near each corner, so it can be hooked over nails driven in the side of the house or partition. This pan being larger at the top than at the bottom may be easily freed from ice by placing it for an instant in a pail of warm water, then inverting it; the ice will slide out at once, leaving the pan ready for use again. This pan is very easily cleaned.

Roosts and Roost Platforms.

The cheapest and one of the most convenient combinations of roost and roost platform is made by nailing cleats to the interior of the rear wall of the house, 2 feet or 2½ feet from the floor and other cleats at the same height, one on each partition. Upon these cleats the platform, which should be made of tongued and grooved boards held together by cross cleats, should rest, but not be nailed. Six inches above the platform a cleat should be nailed to each partition to support the roost. Where one roost is used the platform should be 2 feet wide and the roost 14 inches from the rear wall. Add one foot of width to the platform for each additional roost. The construction is illustrated in Fig. 6.

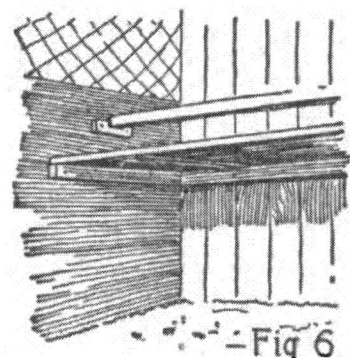

Vermin Proof Roost and Platform.

Fig. 7 illustrates a roost and platform which lice and mites cannot get upon unless carried there by the fowls. It is simply a table 2 feet wide and as long as is necessary to accommodate the flock, with 3-inch wide strips of ⅞ board along the back and across each end to prevent anything falling from it. The front is left open so that droppings may be removed by scraping with a shovel directly into a bucket or box.

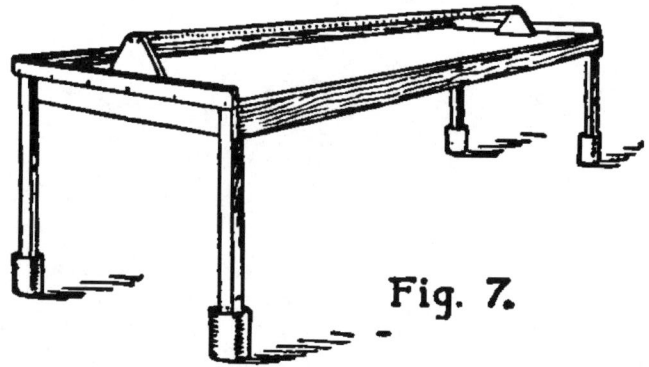

The roost is a piece of 2 x 3 with edges rounded and with pieces of ⅞ board 9 inches high, nailed one to each end to support it. These supports are not nailed to the platform and the roost can be removed when the platform is to be cleaned. Each leg of this table sits in a tin can in which is half an inch or an inch of kerosene, or some other substance which is fatal to lice. If lice or mites get on this roost and platform from the hens they cannot escape after the fowls leave and by spraying the roost and table with liquid lice killer they may be destroyed.

Curtains to Protect the Fowls When on the Roost.

During severely cold weather, especially in buildings having open or cloth fronts, something is needed to protect the fowls during the night when they are on the roost. There are various methods of hanging curtains to serve this purpose, the best of which we illustrate in Fig. 8. Above and 2 or 3 inches in front of the roost platform a strip of board, 6 inches wide, is set edgewise against the underside of the roof or ceiling. To the bottom of this board is tacked cotton cloth, or burlap, of sufficient width so that when dropped the lower edge will be several inches below the platform. At the bottom of this cloth a 2-inch strip should be nailed. When this is let down at night the roosts are inclosed except that a space 2 inches wide in front of the platform is open for the heavy gasses to fall through. In the morning when the caretaker feeds the fowls he rolls up this curtain on the two inch strip and fastens the roll up against the roof, securing it there by a band, one end of which is tacked to the inside of the six inch board and the other hooked to the roof or ceiling in front. Such a curtain should not be made of very heavy or very closely woven material as that will make the roosting quarters too close, causing dampness, and the birds will not obtain sufficient oxygen to breathe.

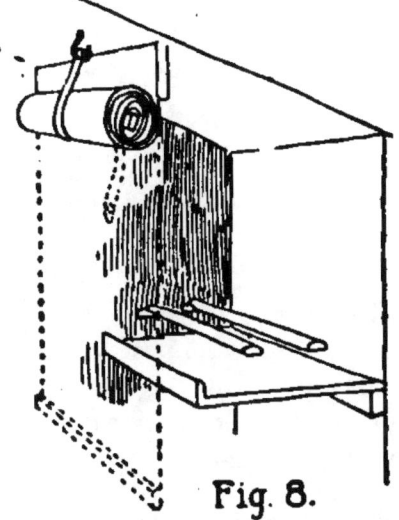

Fig. 8.

A Shelter Tent for Poultry.

In contrast to the roost curtain is a shelter tent (Fig. 9)

which is used to afford the fowls a shady retreat during the hot days of mid-summer. At the corners of a plot of ground 10 feet square, 2 x 2 inch stakes 2 feet long should be driven into the ground until they are firm. Between each pair of

Fig. 9.

these stakes, drive a 2 x 3 stake, 3 feet long, and between each of the three pairs of stakes nail light strips of board parallel to each other. On this frame work stretch a canopy of cotton cloth, burlap or other light material and tack it firmly to the horizontal pieces. When the ground becomes foul under this shelter the stakes can be pulled up and the tent moved to a fresh location.

A Poultry House Awning.

Fig. 10 illustrates the frame for an awning to be built over the windows of a poultry house to prevent the sun shining directly through them into the house in warm weather. The mode of construction is as follows: To the front of the house, at the proper height and about six feet apart, nail light blocks, for example short pieces of 2 x 3 scantling. To these blocks nail strips of inch board 3 or 4 inches wide and four feet long so that they stand perpendicular to the front of the building. The end pieces may be nailed to the ends of the building. Nail to the outer ends of these strips of the same material with an aggregate length equal to that of the building. Now nail a light strip along the adjacent roof, near the edge; if the roof

Fig 10.

is covered with roofing fabric, held in place by cleats, this strip should be nailed through the cleats so that the roofing will not be injured. From this piece to the parallel piece in front nail light pieces three feet apart and the frame is ready for the awning.

Almost any light weight material will do, canvas, cotton cloth, burlap, bran sacks, etc. If this awning is to be used but one season it may be tacked to the frame we have described but if the owner plans to use it a second season it should be made in sections ten or twelve feet long and be tacked to pieces of inch square stuff which can be nailed lightly to the other frame work. At the end of the season these pieces can be detached and the cloth rolled on them and stored. The frame may be left standing for use next season. This frame may be made so as to be easily detachable by fastening it to blocks on the side and roof of the house with screws or bolts.

A Wall Nest.

A convenient nest, which may be hooked to the wall of the pen high enough so that it will not reduce the floor space and which can be readily removed when it is desired to clean it, may be according to Fig. 11. A box about 12 inches wide and 15 inches long by 8 inches deep may rest upon brackets nailed to the wall and be secured by a hook at each end. Such nests may be made in tiers if desired.

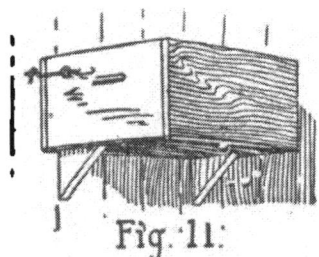

To protect them, a cover may be hinged to the wall at a point several inches above the nests so that it will slant down to the front and prevent any of the fowls roosting there.

A Convenient Arrangement of Fixtures for a House with a Hall Way.

In Fig. 12 is illustrated a manner of placing roosts, roost platforms, nests and feed troughs so that the work of cleaning the platforms, gathering the eggs and feeding and watering the fowls may be done without entering the pens. A represents the roost platform and B the roost; the door, C, is hinged at the top and swings up to permit the care taker to scrape the droppings from the platform into a box held in the alley. Eighteen inches below the roost platform is shelf D, on which the nest boxes rest; door E may be turned up to permit the care taker to gather the eggs or remove the nest boxes to clean them. F is the feed trough which rests upon the floor and which is kept in the alley except when the fowls are eating. At feeding time the trough is filled and pushed through the opening made by raising the door G. The trough should be so high that the fowls cannot get out into the walk over it when it is placed in position. This trough should not extend entirely across the pen but a space should be left for a second door similar to door G, and about a foot long, through which the water fountain may be placed in the pen. In a house thus equipped it is necessary for the attendant to enter the pens only when it is desired to handle some of the birds or to clean the floors. The windows and small doors that open into the yards may be opened by ropes attached to their tops and running over two pulleys to the alley.

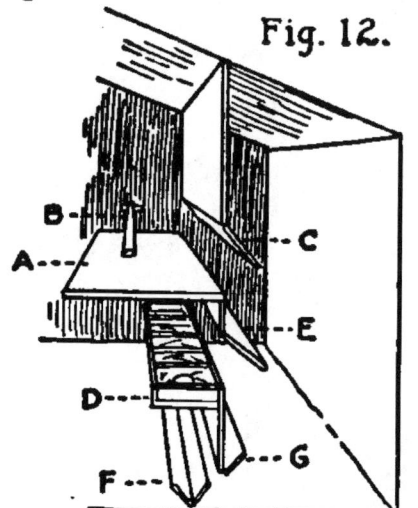

Fig. 12.

Made in the USA
Columbia, SC
15 May 2025

57963751R00057